POLITICS

WEIRD

★★★ O ★★★

PEDIA

POLITICS

WEIRD

★★★ O ★★★

PEDIA

The Ultimate Book of Surprising, Strange, and Incredibly Bizarre Facts about Politics

TIM ROWLAND

Racehorse Publishing

Racehorse Publishing books may be purchased in bulk at special discounts for sales promotion, corporate gifts, fund-raising, or educational purposes. Special editions can also be created to specifications. For details, contact the Special Sales Department, Skyhorse Publishing, 307 West 36th Street, 11th Floor, New York, NY 10018 or info@skyhorsepublishing.com.

Racehorse Publishing™ is a pending trademark of Skyhorse Publishing, Inc.®, a Delaware corporation.

Visit our website at www.skyhorsepublishing.com.

10 9 8 7 6 5 4 3 2 1

Library of Congress Cataloging-in-Publication Data is available on file.

Cover design by Daniel Brount
Cover illustrations by iStockphoto

Print ISBN: 978-1-63158-388-9
Ebook ISBN: 978-1-63158-390-2

Printed in China

To my wife Beth, among whose many talents are organizational and research skills, without which this book would not have been possible.

contents

INTRODUCTION

When the British government ruled India, it became concerned with the number of cobras in the land (the venomous snake being something of a rarity in the British Isles), so the politicians did what any politician would do: set a bounty on the reptile, paying citizens of Delhi for every dead snake they produced. The snake population plunged until residents figured out that they could earn a steady income by breeding cobras, which they duly killed and turned over to the authorities in exchange for cash. When the British government learned of this, it did what any government would do: stopped paying for dead snakes. This left the cobra breeders with a surplus of reptiles, which they simply released back into the streets, leaving the city with far more snakes than it had prior to government intervention. This example has become famous as the Cobra Effect—the tendency of those in power to make bad situations much worse. "Politics," said the publisher Ernest Benn, "is the art of looking for trouble, finding it whether it exists or not, diagnosing it incorrectly, and applying the wrong remedy." As such, politics and government are weird almost by definition.

This book, a desultory collection of curious political anecdotes from around the world, is primarily intended to be fun. Obviously, it is by no means a complete list—that would take a collection of volumes that would fill the mightiest library. Nor is there any pattern or attempt to categorize the snippets beyond the chapter headings, in hopes to keep the book lively. It is also hoped that readers, from time to time, will notice parallels to the modern political condition, which is to say that no matter how extreme things might seem today, we have been here before. (Those who believe Donald Trump is one-of-a-kind have perhaps never studied Andrew Jackson.)

A considerable problem, when dealing with oddball items, is separating truth from legend. (No, contrary to several popular websites, it is not illegal in Liverpool, England, for a woman to be topless in public—except as a clerk in a tropical fish store.) Although relied upon here from time to time for inspiration, Internet lists should generally be considered suspect, for the simple reason that they are in the business of attracting eyeballs, not of conducting scholarly research. That being said, all of history (not just flashy websites) is rife with misconceptions, often perpetuated by those with political agendas. For example, it was in the interest of those who murdered Ludwig II of Bavaria to assign him the sobriquet of the Mad King, and tell all manner of lurid stories about him as an excuse for their power-grab. Sadly, Ludwig's eccentric behavior has been recast through the ages as insanity, even as his fantastic array of castles and theaters are something of a wonder of today's world.

The truth of the tidbits in this book has generally been verified to the highest degree possible. That isn't to say that something didn't slip through the cracks, or that what's accepted as accurate by historians is always accurate. Someone finding an item herein that seems to be too incredible to be true is certainly encouraged to check it out. In this world of dubious social media sites, that's a good habit to be in no matter what the issue. A selected list of books, newspaper articles, and websites are also included in this bibliography (pg. 205) for those interested in learning more.

Who says history and politics are dull?

Still, the overriding theme in this book is that truth is stranger than fiction, and politics is stranger than truth. A decade ago, the government of Bangkok became frustrated that its police officers were taking minor but unsanctioned privileges, such as showing up late for work or parking in reserved spaces. Politicians came up with the idea that officers who were behaving badly would be forced to wear a colorful plaid armband, which would be a symbol of shame and embarrass the officer into maintaining better manners. But almost immediately the plaid armbands became something of a collector's item and/or fashion statement, and the armbands disappeared as fast as they could be produced. This sent administrators back to the drawing board to design a new armband that would be more likely to cause shame and modify the officers' behavior. The result? A pink armband with the Hello Kitty logo.

CHAPTER 1

ON THE CAMPAIGN TRAIL

In the early years of America, begging people for their votes was considered beneath the dignity of a presidential candidate, whose greatness precluded the dirty work of the campaign. It was like the old saw about banks only lending people who didn't need the money; if you needed to ask someone for his vote, you didn't deserve it.

That, obviously, has changed. And more's the pity. Because in those days, resources didn't flow from the people to the candidate; they flowed from the candidate to the people. To be sure, qualifications mattered, sort of, but many an election was determined by which candidate threw the best party. In other words, we chose our presidents in much the same way college kids choose a fraternity.

George Washington was a great man and he won elections because he was a great man. But it didn't hurt that he distilled enough whiskey to float a frigate, and was not shy about ladling it out of the barrel on election day.

> Since the early days of our country, many other things about campaigning have changed—some in ways that are good, some bad, and some just plain weird.

Basil Marceaux, a perennial campaigner for all levels of offices in Tennessee and most recently running in 2018 for governor, hasn't won election, but he *has* won wide acclaim among the national media for his unconventional views. He denied accusations of being drunk in a campaign video, saying his speech was slurred because he only has three teeth.

In response to Russian interference in the 2016 election, the Washington, D.C. city council changed the name of the street where the Russian embassy is located to Boris Nemtsov Plaza, in honor of the Russian opposition leader who was killed outside the Kremlin in 2015. In response, Russia changed the street address of the American embassy in Moscow to 1 North American Dead End.

During the Civil War, there were serious calls for Lincoln to cancel the 1864 election on the grounds of a national emergency. Lincoln wouldn't do it, saying "if the rebellion could force us to forego, or postpone a national election, it might fairly claim to have already conquered and ruined us."

The primary election system in America came about because reformers feared politics had fallen into the hands of party bosses, with diminished citizen influence. Primaries were supposed to return politics to the people. Since primaries were spread throughout the year, the primary system made politics far more expensive than it had been in the past. That's true for the taxpayers as well as for the candidates—in 2016 it cost nearly a half a billion dollars just to administer primary elections in the United States. Many primary elections still don't allow open participation, meaning that many taxpayers are paying for a process in which they are prohibited from participating.

Mark Washburne, a candidate in New Jersey's 11th Congressional District in 2018, had a very bad Election Day. Until he didn't.

The Democrat, who said he would vote to impeach Donald Trump, finished a distant third in the primary. A bit later, however, he discovered the 74 write-in votes he received for mayor in his hometown of Mendham were enough to win him the nomination for that office, where he faced off against Republican Councilwoman Christine Serrano Glassner—whose husband Michael was the 2016 deputy campaign chairman for Donald Trump. Washburne is less known as running for office than he is, well, running. He is president of the US Running Streak Association and the Streak Runners International, and, as of 2018, hasn't missed a day of running since 1989.

Prior to the 1980 presidential debate, someone stole a copy of President Jimmy Carter's briefing notes, which ended up in the hands of challenger Ronald Reagan. So equipped, Reagan handily won the debate with memorable lines like "There you go again," to effectively ward off Carter's pointed attacks on Reagan's record. A 1983 investigation into the purloined prep by the Justice Department produced a 2,400-page document, but no definitive culprit, due to "the professed lack of memory or knowledge on the part of those in possession of the documents." Columnist George Will eventually admitted to an "inappropriate" role in helping Reagan prepare for the debate, but denied having anything to do with the theft. Will wrote Carter that "My cursory glance at it convinced me that it was a crashing bore and next to useless—for you (Carter) or for anyone else." This was in response to Carter's letter to Will, in which the president said he had harbored a resentment toward the columnist, until he read Will's book on baseball, *Men at Work*. "Recently, in order to learn how to be a better Braves fan next year, I spent $1 in a used bookstore for the book, and really enjoyed it," Carter wrote. "Even if the news stories about the debate incident are true, I feel that we are even now."

William "Big Bill" Thompson was Chicago's last Republican mayor, leaving office in 1931. He was also, as a confidante of Al Capone, perhaps the most corrupt Chicago mayor (which is saying something). The *Chicago Tribune* was not a fan, editorializing, "For Chicago, Thompson has meant filth, corruption, obscenity, idiocy, and bankruptcy. . . . He has given the city an international reputation for moronic buffoonery, barbaric crime, triumphant hoodlumism, unchecked graft, and a dejected citizenship." Thompson's corruption was well-known, and he seemed well on his way for defeat in the 1928 mayoral election until he rented a hall and held a "debate" among himself and two live rats that he carried in cages as representation of his opponents. After this the tide turned, and he won the race. Thompson got help from Capone, including the so-called "Pineapple Primaries" in which gangsters disrupted polling places with hand grenades. After his death, two safe deposit boxes were discovered in Thompson's name, containing $1.8 million in cash and securities. As Chairman of the Illinois Waterways Commission, Thompson once (purposefully) attracted copious media coverage by forming an expedition to the South Seas to find a tree-climbing fish.

★

In New Zealand, parliamentary elections can be called by the prime minister, and that's exactly what Robert Muldoon did in 1984 following a mutiny in his own party. The call came at the spur of the moment and when Muldoon was quite clearly drunk. In this instance, liquor and politics didn't mix, as Muldoon lost.

In 2013, police in the South Asian nation of Maldives detained a coconut on suspicion of vote-rigging during a contentious presidential election. The coconut, which was taken into custody after it was discovered outside a public polling place, was suspected of being a tool of magicians who were using it to cast a spell on political opponents. Police said it was not clear which political party the coconut was allied with, but in any event said it was doubtful it would lead to any arrests.

American politics being what they are, it stands to reason that the choice of the federal Election Day—the first Tuesday after the first Monday in November—would not be a simple affair. The choice of Tuesday was relatively straightforward. For religious reasons, voting could not interfere with the weekend. Wednesday was out because that's when goods were sent to market. The polling place, for a farmer, would often take the better part of the day to reach, so he could ride to the voting locale on Monday, vote and return home on Tuesday, and go to market on Wednesday.

Andrew Jackson was the first president to organize what might be thought of as a modern campaign, sending supporters into the field to spread his message. He opened two campaign offices, something that was unheard of at the time. He also had no qualms about awarding federal jobs to those who had helped campaign.

Joe Walsh, maybe best known for his guitar solo on the Eagles song "Hotel California" ran for president in 1980 under the motto "Life's Been Good" with the campaign plank of "free gas for everyone." He was 32 at the time and didn't meet the constitutional requirement that presidents be 35 years of age, so he later ran for Vice President in 1992 with New Orleans songwriter and shaman Goat Carson under the slogan "We Want Our Money Back!"

Will Rogers said, "The trouble with practical jokes is that very often they get elected."

Douglas Stringfellow of Utah had an amazing adventure in WWII. He was wounded by a French landmine and returned home a war hero; he said he was the sole survivor of an Office of Strategic Services espionage unit that was captured and tortured in a concentration camp after parachuting into Germany to kidnap a prominent Nazi nuclear scientist. His heroism helped him win a US House seat in 1952, pulling an upset against a popular incumbent. Campaigning for reelection two years later, he recalled his military service on the television show *This is Your Life*—but the *Army Times* thought it smelled a rat and reported on his inconsistencies. After at first calling the attacks "politically motivated," Stringfellow appeared on television again, this time in tears as he confessed that he made the whole story up.

By today's standards of dark attack ads, the television advertisement created by Georgia gubernatorial candidate Nick Belluso might not seem so bad. Still, in 1978 it was so disturbing that only one station agreed to air it. The spot began with the candidate speaking. "This is Nick Belluso. In the next ten seconds you will be hit with a tremendously hypnotic force. You may wish to turn away. Without further ado let me introduce to you the hypnogenecist of mass hypnosis, the Reverend James G. Masters. Take us away, James." Masters, dressed in wizardly clothing and standing in a rising mist, spoke. "Do not be afraid. I am placing the name of Nick Belluso in your subconscious mind. You will remember this. You will vote on Election Day. You will vote Nick Belluso for governor. You will remember this. You will vote on Election Day. You will vote Nick Belluso for governor." Belluso didn't win, obviously, since so many TV stations were scared of the liability if his stunt actually worked.

By way of a message sent with evangelist Billy Graham, Republican presidential candidate Richard Nixon offered retiring Democratic President Lyndon Johnson shared credit for ending the Vietnam War if he, Johnson, would clandestinely support Nixon's candidacy. Johnson largely did, until it became apparent that Nixon had double-crossed him by sabotaging the Paris Peace Talks.

Voter fraud might be overhyped today, but in the 1940s it was a verified reality. Among the most interesting cases is Lyndon Baines Johnson, who in his first race for US Senate managed to turn a 20,000-vote deficit into an 87-vote win. The larger-than-life Texan was in a Democratic primary runoff against Coke Stevenson, and the facts, agreed upon by both sides, show how difficult it can be to steal an election. The early tally on primary night showed Stevenson with a close, but still comfortable 20,000-vote lead, yet when the vote came in, Johnson had somehow managed to win this time around by a staggering 10,000 votes—perhaps the greatest reversal of electoral fortunes in American history. Post mortems showed that election officials in tiny Alice, Texas, filled in ballots and deposited them in Box 13 for people who had not voted, and then simply changed the number 7 in 765 to a 9, instantly awarding

Johnson an extra 200 votes. When Johnson was attacked for malfeasance, he was defended by attorney Abe Fortes. In 1965 Johnson nominated Fortes to the Supreme Court. Smelling a rat, Stevenson personally visited the town of Alice, taking with him Texas Ranger Frank Hamer, who had led the posse that caught and killed legendary outlaws Bonnie and Clyde. The 200 ballots in question were all in the same handwriting, were written in different color ink than had been filled in by voters who had, miraculously, showed up at the Alice, Texas polling place in alphabetical order.

> While it is broadly acknowledged that Johnson stole the 1948 Senate election, it is also acknowledged that 6 years earlier he had the senatorial election stolen from him.

For South Texas in the 1940s, this was business as usual. In a previous primary, one candidate had won a South Texas county by a vote of 3,000–5. After the candidate had a falling out with the county's party boss, he lost the ensuing runoff by the exact same vote.

These fraudulent votes at least were cast in peace. In Bleeding Kansas, somewhere between 60 and 80 people were killed in the 1850s over votes that would play a role in determining whether Kansas would enter the Union as a free or slave state.

In some elections, subsequent congressional investigations showed that a majority of the voters in Kansas elections weren't even from Kansas. Many voters were from Missouri (where hundreds of pro-slavery men known as Border Ruffians crossed the territorial line to vote), or New England (which sent abolitionists for the same purpose). In one location, 584 of the 604 ballots were fraudulent.

New England settlers were armed with Sharps rifles, sent by Abolitionist Henry Ward Beecher in crates labeled "Bibles."

After Ruffians crossed the border to steal the 1855 election and elect pro-slavery politicians into office—and moved the capital to the Missouri border—free-state abolitionists held their own election and established their own legislature in Topeka. President Franklin Pierce backed the pro-slavery legislature, while a congressional delegation concluded that, had the election been fair, the free-staters would have won.

Democrat Sam Tilden of New York rather handily won the presidential election of 1876 over Ohio's Rutherford B. Hayes. He won by nearly 3 million votes, or 51 percent to 49 percent. He also had a 19-point lead in the electoral college (although four states totaling 20 electoral votes were too close to call), but Hayes became president under the Compromise of 1877, which awarded all 20 electoral votes to Hayes in exchange for the Republican's promise to end Reconstruction. This allowed Southern Democrats to get back to the business of denying black men the vote, which they had guaranteed in the wake of the Civil War.

Hayes's best attribute, in the eyes of one supporter, was that he was "obnoxious to no one." An opposition newspaper editor called him "a very nice, prim, little, withered-up, fidgety old bachelor," which was not a compliment, but not much in the way of an attack, either.

Democrats won the South with help of paramilitary groups keeping blacks from the polls.

★

The small Minnesota town of Dorset chose as its mayor Robert Tufts when he was just three years old. The mayor is selected by drawing names out of a hat. The mayor's motto: "Be nice, and no poopy talk."

"Silent Cal" Coolidge was a taciturn president who answered the question of whether he would run for reelection not by holding a press conference, but by going back to Vermont and buying a house—leaving it to the press to put two and two together.

Coolidge's campaigning was low-key, and so were his politics. Among Coolidge's more remembered contributions to the White House was a recipe for corn muffins.

Coolidge had a curious way of keeping his finger on the pulse of the electorate. At night he would pull his hat down low and wander the streets of Washington, unnoticed, just people-watching. While campaigning was not his style, he did have a sense of mirth. When the Secret Service installed an alarm bell in the Oval Office, Coolidge took a liking to ringing it and then hiding behind a pillar just to watch his protectors' bafflement.

CHAPTER 2
THE POLITICS OF AMERICAN DEMOCRACY

It was the first presidential inauguration, so there were bound to be some hiccups. But under no circumstances can you forget the guest of honor, the president himself. Can you? Well, yes. And perhaps this set the tone for a government that has not always run with seamless precision.

It happened like this: America had a vice president for more than a week before it had a president. John Adams had been sworn in nine days earlier, so he was to do the honors of swearing in George Washington in New York on the thirtieth day of April, 1789. Except Adams didn't know in what capacity he was acting. Maybe it was as vice president, maybe as president of the Senate, maybe as something else. Certainly, everyone wanted Washington's inauguration to be "official," but the framers of the Constitution had left that part out.

And America being America, a squabble immediately arose over the venue of Washington's swearing-in ceremony. The Senators won that round over House objections, so finally everything was ready except—no Washington. In all the hubbub about protocol, someone forgot to send the coach that was to pick him up, delaying the ceremony for more than an hour.

> Washington rode to his inauguration alone. When it was over, he went back to his residence and ate dinner alone as well.

The new president graciously said he would not be in need of a salary if Congress would just pay his expenses. Remembering the copious bills Washington had accumulated during the war, Congress graciously declined.

The first draft of George Washington's original inauguration speech ran 73 pages long, much of it a defense of his decision to take the job. He was saved from himself by James Madison who wrote him a better and far briefer speech.

Hoping to set both an economic and fashion trend, Washington made sure his attire was made in America.

It was only at the last minute that someone decided to add a Bible to Washington's oath. But none were to be found until the Freemasons provided one, simultaneously adding both a religious and conspiratorial component for future generations to argue about.

In England, parliament stood during the king's speeches. In a pointed bit of symbolism, Congress remained seated during Washington's.

The first two men elected to the US Senate were Robert Morris of Philadelphia and William Maclay of Harrisburg, both products of Pennsylvania's electors (the Senate was not yet in the hands of the people). The first two members of the Senate were notable for the degree to which they despised each other. Were it not for each man undercutting the efforts of the other, the nation's capital might well have been located in one of their respective cities.

When we think of American government we often think of transparency. But it was not always so. In its first years of existence, the US Senate met in secret.

The original duties of the Senate doorkeeper were to keep people out of the chamber, along with tending the Senate's two horses and procuring firewood.

Early in the history of our nation, there was an impulse in the Senate toward approving all presidential nominees to public office out of "senatorial courtesy." This courtesy lasted three months. On August 5th, the Senate rejected a Washington appointee to the position of naval officer to the Port of Savannah because a Georgia Senator preferred that the job go to one of his buddies. From that point until the 1930s, the Senate could reject a presidential nomination purely on the grounds of the appointee being "personally obnoxious."

Senator William Blount had a sparkling resume as a Founding Father, having helped to shepherd through the Constitution and give birth to the State of Tennessee. But his land speculations ran him into debt and when he was discovered conspiring with the British to inflate southern land values, he became the first federal official to face impeachment. Blount showed everyone what he thought of that by failing to show up at his Senate trial. Senators lacked a policing force to go get him, so they weaponized the doorman, raised his pay, and the Senate Sergeant at Arms was born. He proved to be a better doorman than lawman, however, and when he failed to track down Blount, the Senate decided that expulsion served its purposes well enough so charges against him were dismissed.

The cornerstone for the US Capitol was laid by George Washington in 1793. Despite subsequent attempts to find it, no one knows where it is.

> **The cornerstone ceremony included a parade, music, and the barbecuing of a five-hundred-pound ox.**

An early concern of Congress was that members might conspire to thwart legislation by agreeing not to show up, thereby denying the necessary quorum, so the Senate passed rules authorizing the use of force to bring missing lawmakers into the chamber. In 1988 Senator Bob Packwood was carried feet first by Capitol Police onto the Senate floor in order to permit a vote on campaign finance reform.

Politicians today who consider the press to be the enemy of the people come by their paranoia honestly. In 1798, the Federalist administration of President John Adams passed the Alien and Sedition Act, threatening to imprison correspondents favorable to Thomas Jefferson's Democratic-Republican Party.

> ## At the time, Jefferson was Adams's vice president.

Trying to bring decorum to the Senate, Jefferson forbade the Senators' custom of "coughing, hissing, or spitting" while another member was speaking.

As president, Jefferson vigorously attacked the judiciary, which he believed was in the pocket of the Federalists. Jefferson's allies in Congress abolished lower courts and terminated judges who had been appointed for life. Supreme Court Justice Samuel Chase was impeached by the House on charges of political bias, but acquitted by the Senate.

The Sedition Acts specifically made it illegal to print anything about Congress that was false or malicious. When Philadelphia editor William Duane printed the contents of a leaked bill—which would have established a partisan (and decidedly unconstitutional) committee to decide which electoral ballots should count—the Federalists got him on a technicality; he wrote in the newspaper that the bill had passed, when in fact it was still pending. Based on this "false" reporting, the Senate Federalists ordered his arrest. The journalist prudently went into hiding until the next election, which went in favor of Jefferson and the Democratic-Republicans; this obviously got him off the hook.

Originally, under the Constitution, designated state electors (not the people) voted for two presidential candidates, making no distinction between president and vice president. The top two vote-getters became president and vice president, meaning the two offices could potentially be filled by heated rivals—as had been the case with Adams and Jefferson.

★

This flaw in the Constitution wasn't discovered until after George Washington left office, and the framers discovered their mistake. In 1796, Adams won a majority of electors, but the Federalist electors split their vote among the remaining Federalist candidates, allowing Jefferson's Democratic Republicans to elevate him to second place.

★

As sparks flew between the two men, the issue was readily apparent; for example, in the European revolutionary wars, Adams openly backed Britain, while Jefferson openly backed France. Internationally, this led to some obvious confusion over just where America stood.

> **The framers drew up the presidential electoral criteria in order to elevate the best men into power and thwart the power of political parties. A good idea, perhaps, but it didn't work.**

In 1800, the Federalists and Democratic Republicans formed rudimentary tickets, John Adams and Charles Pinckney for the Federalists against Thomas Jefferson, and Aaron Burr for the Democratic Republicans. But that didn't work either. Since each elector voted for two men, there was a chance those two men would tie. In 1800 that happened, as Jefferson and Aaron Burr tied for the top spot. This threw the election into the House of

Representatives, where the Federalists tried to make mischief by supporting Burr. Neither man received the required majority through the first 35 ballots, until Alexander Hamilton brokered a deal that gave Jefferson the win.

Burr shot Hamilton to death in a duel four years later.

Were it not for the clause in the Constitution counting slaves as three-fifths of a person for purposes of representation, Adams would have been reelected.

The election, known as the Revolution of 1800, was as nasty as any presidential election today. Everyone seemed to hate everyone. Hamilton wrote a letter criticizing his fellow Federalist Adams that was fifty-four pages long.

The problems exposed by the elections of 1796 and 1800 were patched by the 12th Amendment, which created separate tallies for president and vice president.

Massachusetts didn't ratify the 12th Amendment until 1961.

Aaron Burr, incidentally, was admitted to Princeton at the age of thirteen—as a sophomore. He graduated at age sixteen. He and Hamilton got off on the wrong foot when Burr drew up a charter for a badly needed water company in New York, for which he enlisted Hamilton's support. In the fine print of the water-company charter, there was also a provision for a bank. When the charter was granted, Burr built the bank and scrubbed plans for a water plant. The banker Hamilton understandably felt he had been the victim of the old bait-and-switch.

The idea of a presidential running mate in terms of a vice president wasn't solidified until the Civil War, when Abraham Lincoln ran with Andrew Johnson in 1864. The idea was a harmonious union of the Republican Lincoln with the Democrat Johnson in order to preclude partisan rancor. As Will Rogers said of Communism, it was a good idea, but it didn't work. In the end, Lincoln was assassinated and Johnson was impeached.

Only two US Presidents have returned to serve in Congress, John Quincy Adams and, yes, Andrew Johnson.

During the Civil War, radical Republicans felt that a simple oath of office was not enough, so they initiated an Ironclad Test Oath that was supposed to keep Confederate sympathizers out of office.

At age 28, John Henry Eaton was the youngest person elected to the US Senate—despite the constitutional requirement that Senators be 30 years of age. It is possible that, in those days of spotty record keeping, Eaton did not know his exact age. It is also possible he didn't know of the constitutional requirement. It is equally possible that he knew of both and didn't care. In any event, this detail seemed to have escaped the Senate, which duly swore Eaton into office in 1818.

Through the early years of American democracy, the only real national meeting of the nascent political parties occurred in Congress, and it was these men who selected the presidential candidates. This did not do wonders for the whole separation of powers idea, and indeed, prior to the War of 1812, Senators and Representatives told James Madison he could forget about being nominated for a second term unless he declared war on Great Britain.

Madison, during that war, became the first and last president to lead American troops on a live field of battle. He did not make an overpowering success of it, exiting from the Battle of Bladensburg outside the nation's capital at much faster speeds than he had entered.

In 1870, Joseph Rainey became the first black man to serve in the US House of Representatives, winning a special election in

South Carolina for the seat of the corrupt Benjamin Whittemore, whom Congress had refused to seat. As the South began to regain control of its politics following reconstruction, Rainey was defeated in a reelection bid and Whittemore was elected to the State Senate.

Decades after George Washington's death, Congress was completing work on the rotunda of the US Capitol, and lawmakers wanted something memorable to place in the center. They commissioned American sculptor Horatio Greenough, who delivered his work in 1841. And *memorable* was the word for it. It was a statue of George Washington (fair enough), but what caught people's attention was the attitude in which the great founder was positioned. The twelve ton, ten-foot-high marble depicted a seated Washington in a toga, half nude, with a well-muscled chest and a towel draped over his bicep. Some wags suggested it looked as if the general were getting ready to take a bath. This beefcake version of George didn't play well among the members of Congress, who wanted it gone about two weeks after it had been placed. A couple of years later, they got their way, and the statue was relegated to the Capitol Plaza (which had its own issues). Because it seemed rather rude to ask a naked George to sit out there in the ice and snow, workers were ordered to build him a shed. As anyone who has ever seen an outhouse can attest, this made things much worse. Eventually it was decided that the statue was less a work of art than a museum curiosity—and so today it can be seen in the Smithsonian.

According to Teddy Roosevelt, "When they call the roll in the Senate, the Senators do not know whether to answer 'Present' or 'Not guilty.'"

The record for a Senate filibuster is held by Strom Thurmond, who rambled on for 24 hours and 18 minutes to hold up Civil Rights legislation—it being that important to him that blacks not be viewed on equal terms with whites. Filibuster rules do not allow for bathroom breaks, so Thurmond sweated out extra fluids in a steam room prior to his epic performance, and kept an aide handy with a bucket just in case.

> Thurmond is the only Senator to have served to the age of 100.

Democracy has survived largely through its sense of humor. In 2017, the federal government, in an ongoing crackdown on illegal immigrants, announced the creation of VOICE, the Victims of Immigration Crime Engagement hotline, catering to "the needs of crime victims and their families who have been impacted by crimes committed by removable criminal aliens." The alien hotline was immediately flooded with callers reporting sightings of space invaders, Bigfoot, and other alien phenomena.

The first veto in American history came courtesy of George Washington on April 5th, 1792, who rejected a congressional plan to award an extra representative to populous states that were underrepresented in Congress. Washington's veto was based on a violation of the constitutional principle that no state should receive a delegate in excess of 1 per 30,000 people. But in siding with the rural South, it began a seven-decade battle for supremacy between the agrarian South and industrial North that culminated in the Civil War.

Presidents have always had uneasy relationships with their generals. When Harry Truman relieved General Douglas McArthur during the Korean war, he said, "I fired him because he wouldn't respect the authority of the President. I didn't fire him because he was a dumb son of a bitch, although he was, but that's not against the law for generals. If it was, half to three-quarters of them would be in jail."

In 1962, JFK chose the font for the fuselage of Air Force One, patterning it after an early printing of the US Constitution.

CHAPTER 3
MONEY POLITICS

For generations it has been axiomatic in politics, as in life, that "the answer to all your questions is money." Even in the days that predated money, it could be said that time was money, and the leaders of early civilizations were the ones who could organize their people and put them to work performing some outsized task building monoliths. As great as Julius Caesar was politically, his bank account did not match his own opinion of his political worth. When captured by pirates who offered his return for 25 talents of silver, Caesar was enraged and demanded that they ask for 50. His inheritance having been confiscated, he was reduced to living in a modest home in a lower middle-class neighborhood prior to his ascension.

Deeply in debt (Caesar, like many politicians, was better at spending than saving), he hitched his political star to Crassus, one of the richest men in Rome. Crassus had made his money by running Rome's fire department, which he turned into the ultimate political cash cow. As the building burned, Crassus negotiated with the property owner over how much he would need to put the fire out. Often, he would accept the deed to the home as payment, turning the owner into one of Crassus's many tenants.

Money, of course, touches all political arenas, not just campaigning. From appropriations for the tiniest of pork barrel projects to bragging rights over the relative wealth of nations, politics and money are intricately entwined. Perhaps no one understood this better than Mark Hannah, the man whose fundraising genius led to the successful candidacies of President William McKinley. "There are two things that are important in politics," Hannah said. "The first is money, and I forget what the second one is."

While we expect politicians to be good stewards of our money, it is rather remarkable and startling how many have been so bad at handling their own. When he died, Alexander Hamilton was so deeply in debt that his funeral doubled as something of an early GoFundMe campaign to pay the costs of his burial.

Hamilton was that rare breed that was better at handling public money than his own. He put young America on solid financial footing, but the salary he was paid to do so did not keep up with his copious expenses which included 7 children and 2 mistresses.

Before becoming the leader of the Revolution, George Washington's success in politics was made possible by his success in business. While other planters such as Thomas Jefferson stubbornly stuck with once-lucrative tobacco, even after the market crashed, Washington switched to wheat. He sold his best product to the Europeans while passing off inferior crops to his neighbors who in turn passed it off to their slaves.

> **Bad money management infuriated Washington, and he could be ruthless when it came to finances. He once even evicted a group of his former Revolutionary War soldiers when they became delinquent on property he was renting to them.**

While there were no Super PACS in the 1700s, wealth still played a role in politics. To win a seat in the Virginia House of Burgesses, George Washington enticed the voters with money, a fiddler, and a healthy swig of rum punch.

> Candidates in those days were
> not accused of vote-buying.
> Instead, it was felt that those who
> held public office were merely
> "generous gentlemen."

James Madison turned up his nose and money-politics in his race for the Virginia House of Delegates, believing it to be improper. He lost.

By the mid-1800s, the average presidential campaign cost $100,000.

In today's dollars, a presidential election in 1850 would have cost $6 million. In 2016, the presidential election for both candidates came to $2.4 billion.

By the mid-1800s, money was becoming an essential part of politics, and a ready source was the government workforce. Politicians felt no shame in shaking down workers for cash, and in 1867, Congress passed a law prohibiting officers and employees of the federal government from soliciting money for political campaigns from naval yard workers.

It seems quaint by today's standards, but in 1921, Truman Handy Newberry spent the modern equivalent of $1.1 million to win a Michigan US Senate seat. The man he beat, however, was automaker Henry Ford, who didn't take the loss lightly and pulled some strings to get Newberry convicted of violating campaign finance laws that had been passed a decade prior. Newberry's conviction was overturned by the Supreme Court, but Congress opened its own inquiry into what at the time seemed like an obscene amount of money in politics, and Newberry resigned.

There's a reason that corporations are so anxious to spend money in politics. Studies have shown a company can expect a 22,000 percent return on their lobbying dollars.

In 2000, one-fourth of 1 percent of the American people gave 68 percent of congressional campaign money.

The US isn't the only country with money-politics issues. In Brazil in 2017, authorities got a tip about corruption, which led them to an apartment where they expected to find computer records and documents. Instead, the otherwise empty flat contained suitcases filled with $16 million in cash. According to the *Washington Post*, "Corruption has been an endemic problem in Brazil for centuries, but a massive investigation has unexplained piles of cash popping up around the country like never before." In 2016, fishermen found hundreds of thousands of dollars floating in the Rio de Janeiro bay.

Nowhere did money and politics swim more in the same waters than in America's Civil War. Abraham Lincoln was known, of course, as "Honest Abe." But when circumstances required, he could also have been called "Practical Abe." Unlike many politicians, Lincoln was good with money both before and after entering politics. He saved most of his own salary and when he died there were 3 uncashed paychecks in his desk drawer. He found it abhorrent that his own wife was blowing her budget for redecorating the presidential mansion, while soldiers were shivering away in their camps with scarcely a warm blanket to their names. He cut her off saying there would be no more money for "flub dubs for that damned house!"

★

The influence of the people on presidential elections began to diminish with the onset of the Industrial Revolution, when business began to underwrite the cost of campaigns in exchange for the expectation of political favors.

Residents of the Ohio River town of Vulcan lost patience with their state government, which for 2 long years failed to replace a collapsed bridge that was the only legal ingress and egress to the community. In frustration, the acting mayor wrote to the Soviet Union and East Germany in 1977, asking for financial assistance to replace the bridge. A Soviet journalist was dispatched to investigate, and within an hour of his arrival the West Virginia Legislature had appropriated $1.3 million for a new bridge.

Former Alaska Senator Ted Stevens was responsible for one of the most egregious pork barrel projects in American history: a $223 million bridge to an island with a population of fifty people.

In 1930, a simple funding request by the House of Representatives cafeteria turned into one of the more rabid debates in congressional history, which is saying something. Rising to defend the funding increase, Representative Charles Underhill of Massachusetts produced two club sandwiches: one from the House cafeteria, one from a local restaurant. The House sandwich compared quite favorably. "Look at the size of this piece of chicken and compare it with this piece of chicken in our own restaurant, and with this larger piece of chicken, a large piece of toast, more mayonnaise, tomato and lettuce, we get only five cents more for our sandwich," he said. Ohio's Frank Murphy, however, used the opportunity to air his grievances against the cafeteria, including the fact that it had stopped serving cheese with its pie. The issue got quite heated, even with the attempted levity of one congressman who rose to ask what members who could not afford such a grand sandwich were expected to eat, and a Massachusetts lawmaker who wanted to know when the cafeteria was going to start serving Boston baked beans and New England boiled dinners. The fiasco was covered in the papers the next day, but the congressmen, apparently not proud of their performance, had the debate scrubbed from the Congressional Record.

The United States is doing its best to turn the Afghanistan Army into a professional unit. That includes matching uniforms, which cost American taxpayers $28 million in 2017. Unfortunately, the US allowed the Afghani defense minister to pick the camouflage design, which he chose out of a catalog because it was pretty. It might have looked good, but the pattern was a forest green and largely ineffective in a country that is 98 percent desert.

The federal government owns an estimated 77,000 buildings that are nearly or totally empty. These unused buildings cost $1.7 billion in basic maintenance costs, and the government would like to do something about it but is not able to because there is no reliable centralized database of these properties.

> In 2018, US House candidates raised more campaign cash by August 27th than they raised during the entire 2014 midterm election cycle.

The candidate that raises the most money wins 90 percent of the time. The only election cycle in modern history in which this was not true was 2010. Then, the candidate who raised the most money won 86 percent of the time.

★

Taxpayer money is often criticized for the projects upon which it is spent, but sometimes the money never makes it to its intended purpose. In the Civil War, conventional wisdom has always held that the South was poorly equipped and poorly fed. But early on, it was Union troops who had worms in their food and were issued uniforms and shoes that fell apart in the rain—because military contractors kept much of the appropriated money for themselves.

Politicians argue over the relative wealth of their nations, but the answer depends on how the question is asked. Per capita, Qatar is the wealthiest with a GDP of $146,000 per person. Qatar's unemployment rate is 0.1 percent, no one lives below the poverty level, and 1 in 6 residents is a millionaire.

China had the largest world GDP at $17.6 trillion, but with its mammoth population it only ranks as the 87th wealthiest nation.

Judged by natural resources, Russia is the wealthiest nation. It has $76 trillion in natural resources, including $19 trillion worth of natural gas and $28 trillion worth of timber.

By 2010, wars in Iraq and Afghanistan had cost the United States $1.6 trillion.

There are competing stories as to how "pork barrel" came to mean public graft. Some said a barrel of pork was given to slaves, who were left to fight for the largest share. But more generally, a pork barrel was synonymous with wealth. James Fennimore Cooper wrote, "I hold a family to be in a desperate way, when the mother can see the bottom of the pork barrel."

CHAPTER 4
POLITICAL ANIMALS

From parades to pets, animals have played a supporting and symbolic role in politics. The most familiar animals in American politics are the GOP elephant and the Democratic donkey. The obvious first question when considering these two beasts and the parties they represent is: What politician would want to be associated with a jackass? Andrew Jackson would be the answer to that one, and some historians would acknowledge that the 7th US president had tendencies in that direction.

In fact, during the 1828 presidential election, Jackson's opponents derided him as a jackass, but rather than be offended, Old Hickory embraced the sobriquet. He gave the donkey an extreme makeover, portraying it as resolute, determined, and purposeful with a keen sense of injustice that would not sacrifice its principles.

Disappointed, his enemies dropped the association, and the donkey didn't make another appearance until cartoonist Thomas Nast used the jackass for Democratic institutions beginning in 1870—and not in a good way.

Nast was also responsible for the Republican elephant, and this was not intended as a flattering comparison either. In Nast's 1874 cartoon for *Harper's Weekly*, he insinuated that the elephant was stampeding toward chaos, driven there by a donkey made to look fiercer than it was by donning the skin of a lion. Elephants have been said to be scared of mice, despite their imposing size, and this might have been the cartoonist's way of saying the GOP needed to grow a spine.

Boston Curtis sounds like a name that's so good it must have been made up. That's because it was. Despite that, Boston, or Mr. Curtis, was elected precinct captain in Milton, Washington during the 1938 Republican primary. He received 51 votes, despite the fact that he was a mule. The stunt was arranged by the town's naughty Democratic mayor, Kenneth Simmons, who wanted to prove Republicans were so gullible they would vote for anyone. The election papers bore the hoofprint of the Milton Mule, whose name was Boston and whose owner's name was Curtis.

" Watching politicians create law is, the saying goes, as savory as watching the creation of sausage. But were the two ever combined? Sort of, as a dog named Sausage (Saucisse in French) ran for mayor of Marseille in 2001, and came in 6th, with 4.5 percent of the vote. The dachshund's popularity stemmed from his role as a character in the novels of French writer Serge Scotto. "

In World War II, the Soviet Union trained 40,000 "anti-tank dogs" that were supposed to drop bombs beneath advancing German tanks before returning to the Russian lines. When this didn't work, the Soviets tried to arm the bombs with a detonating device that would go off when the dogs ran under the tank. The anti-tank dogs would up killing more Soviets than Germans because while the dogs had been trained to run under idling tanks, they had not been trained to negotiate a moving tank. Nor, due to costs, had they been trained to tolerate the sound of ammunition, so before the dogs could reach the enemy, they became frightened and ran back to the Soviet lines where the bombs would explode. The Soviets had also trained the dogs using their own diesel-engine tanks, not realizing that dogs, with their keen sense of smell, would distinguish between these and the German tanks that ran on gasoline engines. Too often the bomb-carrying dogs would run to the familiar smell of the diesel fumes. The dogs also played into the hands of German propagandists, who claimed that the Russian men were too scared to fight so they sent their dogs into the fray instead.

Henry Clay is famous enough in American politics, Clay Henry not so much. But the Mayor of Lejitas, Texas, until 1992, had something of a cult following, partly because he could put away as much as a case and a half of beer a day. And partly because he was a goat. Being incorporated, the title of mayor in Lejitas is ceremonial, so the only duty of Clay Henry and his descendants is to attract tourists.

The Roman Emperor Caligula toyed with the idea of naming his horse Incitatus a consul. This, in theory, would allow the horse to send out invitations to state dinners, which would create enough awkward moments so as to be wildly amusing. Or maybe it was just a way to suggest that his contemporary politicians were on par with a horse's patoot. Or maybe Caligula never suggested any such thing (or if he did, only after a bottle or two of wine).

Honeybees have friends in high places. America's Second Lady Karen Pence is a champion of bees, and not without reason. She noted, upon unveiling a hive at the vice-presidential residence, that "One out of three bites of food taken in this country are made possible with the help of pollinators," and that pollinators add at least $15 billion in crop value per year.

Five Arabian mares are celebrated in Islamic legend. It was said that Mohammad, after a brutally fatiguing day in the hot desert, turned his considerable herd of horses loose so they could run to an oasis. Halfway there, he called them back. Only 5 mares were disciplined enough to listen, and these were the foundation of the Arabian herd that bolstered the fortunes of the Ottoman Empire.

In the Brazilian city of Sao Paulo in 1958, corruption was so rampant that the people elected a black rhinoceros named Cacareco to city council. The animal received more than 100,000 votes, winning in a landslide—or maybe a mudslide—but city officials refused to certify her election. Cacareco was the inspiration behind the Rhinoceros Party of Canada, which survived for 30 years, until 1993.

> The Rhinoceros Party made one promise, and that was to break all its promises. Among these promises was to store nuclear waste in the Senate, and to end crime by abolishing all laws.

Rhinoceros Party candidates never win, but they cause some embarrassment when their candidates—including a clown named Tickles—finish ahead of established politicians. Former Major League Pitcher Bill "Spaceman" Lee ran for president of the United States as a member of the Rhino party.

The counterculture of the 1960s had a notably low opinion of politicians, and in 1968 they announced that a 145-pound hog named Pigasus would be the presidential candidate of the Yippies (Youth International Party). Pigasus's candidacy never got past his nomination speech as he and 7 counterculture protesters were arrested in Chicago. As they awaited bail, an officer told the protesters they would be jailed for life because "the pig squealed."

The town of Xalapa in Mexico had a rat problem, so when established politicians failed to do anything about it, voters in 2013 nominated a cat for mayor. The cat had 150,000 Facebook likes and 7,000 votes, but his candidacy was disallowed.

One of the more interesting presidential menageries was in the possession of President Calvin Coolidge. So reticent was Coolidge that he became known as Silent Cal Coolidge. He felt that words were of such importance that he only used them when absolutely necessary. His opponents felt he didn't say much because he seldom grasped the situation at hand.

Among President Coolidge's pets were collies and terriers, but he also had a soft spot for birds. He had a goose named Enoch, a thrush named Old Bill, and two canaries named Nip and Tuck.

Coolidge's white goose was a gift from actress Marie Dressler, who was performing in the Broadway show, *The Goose Woman*. Enoch was unimpressed with its famous owners. When a caretaker left the door to its coop open, the goose flew off and disappeared.

★

Knowing his affinity for animals, foreign dignitaries gave Coolidge two lion cubs (named Tax Reduction and Budget Bureau), a wallaby, and a pigmy hippo.

> For exercise, Coolidge donned a cowboy hat and rode a mechanical horse.

Among the pets of Teddy Roosevelt and his children were numerous dogs, two kangaroo rats and a snake named Emily Spinach.

Benjamin Harrison enjoyed two pet possums, named Mr. Protection and Mr. Reciprocity.

John Tyler tried to breed canaries before figuring out that his breeding pair included two boys. When Tyler's horse General died, the tombstone read: "For twenty years he bore me around the circuit of my practice, and in all that time he never made a blunder. Would that his master could say the same!"

When Donald Trump became entangled in the ever-popular Emoluments Clause, it was the first time many Americans had heard of the Constitutional provision that prevents foreign heads of state from lavishing gifts on US statesmen. But early in the nation's history, the issue came up with some frequency. Andrew Jackson was not permitted to keep a gold medal, a present from Simon Bolivar, and Abraham Lincoln had to turn over a sword and two elephant tusks gifted from the King of Siam, but perhaps the most problematic gift was a pair of lions given to Martin Van Buren by the sultan of Morocco. The presentation was made to an American consul in Tangier, who protested that he could not accept the gift—for reasons, no doubt, that went beyond a simple conflict of interest. The emissary who brought the beasts said he had to deliver them successfully, or it would cause a diplomatic incident that would cost him his head. The lions were given a room at the American embassy while Congress mulled over what to do. Eventually it was decided that the lions could be brought to America, but once here they would have to be auctioned off. They were, fetching a price of $375.

> James Polk, according to family lore, learned to ride a horse before he learned to walk.

President Jackson had a number of horses, but also a parrot named Poll that he taught, intentionally or unintentionally, to swear. At Jackson's funeral, the parrot, apparently distraught by all the commotion, began to curse with such volume and enthusiasm that he had to be carried from the room.

John Quincy Adams supposedly had a pet alligator, given to him by the Marquis de Lafayette. The reptile, the story goes, was kept in a White House bathroom, where it inspired considerable consternation among the guests. If there's any truth to this story it most likely stemmed from when Lafayette was a guest of Adams's in the summer of 1825. In Lafayette's possession was a number of gifts he had been given while touring America, including, perhaps, the gator in question. Lafayette's gifts, during his White House stay, were piled in the East Room; if there was an alligator, it was probably stored there, in the tub of an unfinished bathroom.

Lyndon B. Johnson had been hosting a meeting on foreign investment when he decided to take a break with his two beagles, Him and Her. To give his guests an idea of the dog's "voice," he lifted Him up onto his hind feet by the ears. The vignette went unremarked upon at the time, but a photographer from *Life* magazine recorded the moment, and when the picture was published it caused uproar among the public. Johnson apologized, but was privately baffled, since he's been performing the ear trick with Him since he was a pup and "he seemed to like it."

> It did not end well for Him and Her. Both died young. Her swallowed a rock, and a member of the Secret Service hit Him with a car as the dog was racing across the White House grounds in pursuit of a squirrel.

Presidential candidate Mitt Romney found himself in hot water similar to LBJ, when it surfaced that on a family vacation he had transported his Irish Setter on the roof of his car for 12 hours. The crate was equipped with a windscreen, but animal rights activists and political opponents accused Romney of animal cruelty. The incident of course became the subject of political polling which found that 74 percent of Democrats, 66 percent of Independents, and 63 percent of Republicans consider it inhumane to put a family dog in a kennel on the roof of a car.

Sometimes politicians have been able to turn animal angst to their advantage. Consider Franklin D. Roosevelt, who, on a trip back to the mainland from Hawaii made a stop in the Aleutian Islands. A story evolved that FDR's dog Fala had been left behind on an island, and that a Navy destroyer had been dispatched to retrieve the pet at a cost of $20,000, a sum that Republicans soon inflated to $20 million. Battered by 4 years of war, Roosevelt was seen as vulnerable—at least until he walked into a Teamsters union hall to make a speech on labor issues. Instead, he talked about his dog:

"These Republican leaders have not been content with the attacks on me, or my wife, or on my sons. No, not content with that, they now include my little dog, Fala. Well, of course, I don't resent attacks, and my family doesn't resent attacks, but Fala does resent them. You know, Fala is Scotch, and being a Scottie, as soon as he learned that the Republican fiction writers in Congress had concocted a story that I had left him behind on the Aleutian Islands and sent a destroyer back to find him—at a cost to taxpayers of 2 or 3, or 20 million dollars—his Scotch soul was furious. He has not been the same dog since."

★

The "Fala Speech" is credited in some circles as being the turning point of the campaign. Republicans were seen as attacking the poor little pup, who became a happy, tail-wagging icon as portrayed by wartime cartoonists. FDR won reelection comfortably.

Fala was inconsolable upon Roosevelt's death, racing through a screen door and barking frantically. He attended the funeral and died on the seventh anniversary of FDR's death. His obit appeared on the front page of the *New York Times*, which remembered "the rakish little black Scotty who sat in on the making of history."

> **Fala is the only dog memorialized on the National Mall in Washington, D.C.**

Other dogs have been witnesses to events on the world stage including Russian President Vladimir Putin's black lab Koni, who was a regular at meetings with world leaders. One world leader who was not amused was German Chancellor Angela Merkel, who fears dogs after having been bitten as a child. During a meeting between the two leaders, Putin made a point of giving Koni access and appeared amused by the German leader's discomfort.

Putin once received a tiger cub as a gift, but refused to say who gave it to him or why.

The mother of the former mayor of London Ken Livingstone was afraid he would be a failure because he paid less attention to his studies than he did to his pet lizard.

Despite their roles as Cold War adversaries, Soviet Chairman Nikita Khrushchev and US President John F. Kennedy maintained surprisingly cordial connections. Once, while sitting next to the premier at a state dinner in Vienna, Jackie Kennedy asked about Strelka, the dog the Russians had shot into space. Some months later, Khrushchev sent the Kennedys one of the dog's puppies named Pushinka (Russian for Fluffy). In a letter of thanks, Kennedy wrote, "Mrs. Kennedy and I were particularly pleased to receive 'Pushinka.' Her flight from the Soviet Union to the United States was not as dramatic as the flight of her mother, nevertheless it was a long voyage and she stood it well. We both appreciate your remembering these matters in your busy life." The Cuban Missile Crisis occurred sixteen months later.

Pushinka had puppies, courtesy of the family's Welsh terrier, which the family decided to give away. More than 5,000 Americans wrote to the White House asking for one of the pups.

When French troops helped the government of Mali beat back a terrorist attack, French President Francois Hollande was rewarded by the Malian government with the gift of a dromedary camel.

Unprepared for the logistics involved in handling such a present, it was left in the care of a local family that—presumably not understanding that the animal was a matter of statesmanship—promptly slaughtered it and cooked it in a stew.

Another international traveler, Chi Chi the giant panda who was born in China, was rejected by Moscow after she failed to mate. She wound up at the London Zoo in 1958 and until her death in 1972 was England's best-loved zoo animal. She had been scheduled to be re homed in a zoo in Illinois, but the United States government decided it didn't want to import anything from the Communists, no matter how cute.

The newly designed Enfield rifle was the spark that touched off the Indian Rebellion of 1857, in which Hindu and Muslim sepoys became fed up with British rule. The muzzle-loading rifle, with its tighter tolerances, required its cartridges be greased in order for them to be rammed down the barrel. Among the sepoys, rumor spread that the cartridges, which had to be bitten open, were greased with cow fat, which offended the Hindus, and pig fat, which offended the Muslims.

Along the 1,300-mile border between India and Bangladesh there is an immigration problem. Not with people, but with cows. Cattle cannot be slaughtered or exported in India, but if successfully smuggled across the border they can bring four times the price they command in India. Each year hundreds of thousands of cows are smuggled across the border, setting up a cat-and-mouse game between those trying to cross, and the Indian government trying to catch them before they do.

CHAPTER 5
POLITICAL SECRETS

When they're not in front of the cameras flashing their toothpaste smiles, politicians love to operate in secret—probably to cover up their weirdness. Sometimes the motivation behind the secrecy is sinister, and at other times it's harmless, if misguided. But sometimes the secrecy is difficult to categorize. Take the case of Bohemian Grove, which began as an artists' camp established among the California Redwoods in 1878. It was taken over by San Francisco businessmen early on, and morphed into a club that included most of the past century's Republican presidents and GOP elite. For 2 weeks each summer, important men from around the world are invited to participate in a secret getaway, leading conspiracy theorists to suggest this is where the top-level political and business decisions are formulated sans democratic input.

Or not. In 1989, *Spy* magazine correspondent Philip Weiss infiltrated the club, writing "The religion they consecrate is right-wing, laissez-faire, and quintessentially western, with some Druid tree worship thrown in for fun." The group is supposed to leave business at the door, its members instead focused on mock ritual, music, plays, and no shortage of gin. Weiss wrote, "You know you are inside the Bohemian Grove when you come down a trail in the woods and hear piano music from amid a group of tents and then 'round a bend to see a man with a beer in one hand and his penis in the other, urinating into the bushes."

Despite the edict against conducting business, many deals do occur. Most famous is development of the Manhattan Project that led to development of the atomic bomb.

The Moynahan Commission, formed to examine the excesses of government secrecy, determined in the early 1990s that over the past 25 years, 1.5 billion documents had been classified.

In the 1950s the Labor department refused to disclose how much peanut butter had been purchased by the Army.

The word "classified" didn't come to mean "secret" until 1940.

In a 1974 classified report, the CIA redacted news that terrorists in the "Group of the Martyr Ebenezer Scrooge" planned to sabotage the December 24th flight of "Prime Minister and Chief Courier S. Claus."

In 2011, the CIA declassified a formula for invisible ink used a century ago: a toothpick dipped in milk, the text being visible when later heated "with a flatiron."

There were secret plans in 1962 to attack American planes and ships, engage in military actions against the US, and initiate terrorist campaigns against Miami and Washington, D.C. These plans were not developed by an American enemy, but by the US military itself. These "false flag" attacks, known as Operation Northwoods, would be blamed on the Cuban government, which would give American politicians the pretense for going to war against Cuba and its Communist government. The scheme was rejected by President Kennedy.

Had the attacks taken place, it would have been history repeating itself, in a sense. An accidental explosion that sank the USS

Maine in Havana Harbor in 1898 was blamed on Spain, and used as an excuse to attack Cuba.

When the Mercury spacecraft took astronaut John Glenn into space in 1962, Operation Dirty Trick provided that, if it failed, the Cubans could be blamed by claiming they had utilized electronic interference to bring down the craft. The flight did not fail.

From 1960 to 1965, the United States concocted several plots to assassinate problematic dictator Fidel Castro. Exploding cigars, poison pills, and contaminated air were all considered, as was damaging Castro's image by secreting a chemical in his shoes that would make his beard fall out. But the wackiest plan was to take advantage of Castro's love of skin diving. The plan was to stuff a particularly attractive mollusk full of explosives in hopes Castro would grab it.

Unthinkable as it seems that the government would attack its own people, the CIA's program MKUltra experimented on its own people to identify drugs and physical manipulation, including sex abuse, that could be used in mind control The ultimate goal was to find a "truth serum" to use on Soviet spies. Conversely, there were also attempts to develop knockout drugs and drugs that would cause permanent amnesia. It was even thought that techniques might be found to program minds of people who would be used to carry out assassination plots. The human guinea pigs were citizens of both the US and Canada. The experiments, which were not phased out until 1973, were generally carried out on mental patients, prisoners, drug addicts, and sex workers without their knowledge or consent.

Not all victims were ne'er-do-wells. Frank Olsen, a germ-warfare CIA scientist who worked at Fort Detrick in Maryland, jumped to his death 9 days after his boss gave him LSD without his knowledge. The family was convinced Olsen had been assassinated by the CIA. While the courts refused to let a lawsuit commence on legal grounds in 2013, the judge noted "While the court must limit its analysis to the four corners of the complaint, the skeptical reader may wish to know that the public record supports many of the allegations (in the family's suit), farfetched as they may sound."

> There likely were many other deaths caused by MKUltra, but the true scope of the program will never be known because the CIA destroyed all records of the experimentation.

From 1953 to 1973, in defiance of the Supreme Court, the CIA screened 28 million letters and opened more than 200,000 pieces of mail. The operation ostensibly targeted mail headed overseas for the purposes of national defense, but the mail to and from citizens such as Bella Abzug, Hubert Humphrey, Martin Luther King, Bobby Fischer, and John Steinbeck was opened as well.

In a story that reeked of a Tom Clancy novel, the CIA tried to steal a Soviet submarine that sank in the Pacific in 1968 under 3 miles of water. The CIA spent $200 million building a special ship to pull the sub from the ocean floor, but it broke in half and the agency failed in its primary goal of recovering Soviet nuclear codes and missiles.

The 2017 Wikileaks document dump suggested the CIA has the capability to spy on homes with smart TVs, even when they are turned off. The agency also tinkered with hacking into automobile computers in order to cause crashes, which would allow them to conduct "nearly undetectable" assassinations.

Frank Baum's *Wizard of Oz*, according to historian Henry Littlefield, was in fact a concealed political totem telling the story of 1890s American populism. Littlefield presented the story as an allegory about American monetary policy utilizing the following symbols: Dorothy was the naïve American public; the ruby slippers (silver in the book) represented free-silver monetary policy; the yellow brick road was the gold standard; Oz was the abbreviation for ounce (of gold or silver); the Emerald City was the mirage greenback; and the wizard was the politician, all smoke and mirrors with little real power.

Others have seen the Tin Man as a dehumanized factory man turned into a machine—his lost heart being lost faith in the American economy; the Scarecrow is an American farmer, who is smarter than society believed, and the Cowardly Lion is the populist William Jennings Bryan. In this version, the tornado is the social revolution that changes the world from black and white to color.

Nothing says "government secrets" like UFOs. And nothing says UFOs like Area 51, the barren strip of Nevada landscape where crashed alien spaceships were, according to lore, secreted away. In fact, the government had some interest in allowing this story to spread, since it deflected attention from the base's true use: the development and testing of highly classified spy planes.

The UFO story was given credence by commercial airline pilots who saw crafts flying at 60,000 feet, 4 miles higher than any plane was known to fly. What they were seeing was the high-altitude U-2 spy plane.

★

Although the Area 51 origin myth dates back to the 1947 crash near Roswell, New Mexico of a high-altitude balloon sniffing for nuclear radiation from Soviet bomb tests, the story didn't gain traction until the late 1980s when a man claimed to have reverse-engineered spacecraft at the site. He was later discovered to have faked his credentials, but the myth lived on.

> To the west of Area 51 is the Alien Cathouse, a sci-fi themed brothel promising a "discreet and heavenly close encounter."

A more compelling UFO story came from Clarence S. Chiles and John B. Whitted, two Eastern Airline pilots who claimed to have seen a UFO over Montgomery, Alabama. Their claim of a brightly lit, cigar-shaped craft was taken seriously enough that an investigation was launched, called "Estimate of the Situation." The pilots were deemed credible, but the Air Force hierarchy later had the report destroyed. It's believed today that the pilots saw a type of meteor.

No less a statesman than Britain's former Prime Minister Winston Churchill was dogged by questions of UFOs. In a cache of papers released in 1999 were letters written by the grandson of a man in the Royal Air Force who had served as one of Churchill's bodyguards. The story, admittedly second- or third-hand, was that the prime minister was so alarmed by a RAF encounter with a UFO that he feared "mass panic" among the public, and ordered a 50-year classification on the information. If that's true, it never was and never will be released, since the government did not keep its UFO files accumulated before 1967. It is known, however, that Churchill ordered a study on flying saucers in 1952.

★

Not all presidential secrets involved vital matters of state. Lyndon B. Johnson was known to take a car full of passengers on a joy ride, and as he was careening down a hill toward a lake, he would radio a member of the Secret Service making sure they'd had a chance to fix the brakes. As the car sped toward the water, the flustered Secret Serviceman would confess that there just hadn't been time, but promised to get to it in the coming week. Johnson would shout at him for his ineptitude as the car, full of screaming passengers, plunged into the lake. Johnson's secret was that he was driving a 1962 Amphicar, an amphibious automobile he had been given as a gift—and had no other particular use for.

★

Britain's highly secretive MI6 intelligence agency hacked into an al-Qaeda website and replaced a set of instructions for making a bomb with a recipe for cupcakes.

In the 1950s, the federal government wanted to know the effects of nuclear radiation, so it stole tissue from 900 human cadavers without knowledge or permission of family members. In 1994, President Clinton ordered a report, which in 900 pages acknowledged the clandestine program, which had somewhat euphemistically been called Project Sunshine.

After the horrors of WWII, all things Nazi were verboten—almost. The American government felt that some German scientists and engineers might be of use, so the Joint Intelligence Objectives Agency falsified the records of 1,500 Germans—some likely guilty of war crimes—so they could go to work for the US.

Long before the notorious Plumbers of the Nixon Administration spied on the American public, the inhabitants of Camelot were doing the exact same thing. According to Oval Office tapes of the Kennedy White House, the CIA was called on to wiretap journalists. The plan, code named Mockingbird, listened in on the conversations of several journalists after the press reported on Soviet efforts to fortify their nuclear missile bunkers. The action violated the CIA charter, which strictly prohibited spying on American citizens, but Kennedy's precedent has since been used as justification for domestic spying by Presidents Johnson, Nixon, and George W. Bush.

America's first female president, arguably, was Edith Wilson, the second wife of President Woodrow Wilson. It was not a result anyone wanted or anticipated. Wilson became infatuated with Edith Galt soon after the death of his first wife—too soon to suit his advisors, who feared the nation would be shocked, and that the scandal would cost him reelection. His advisors were so alarmed that they secretly wrote phantom love letters, ostensibly from Wilson to an old lover, and leaked them to the press. Galt was not dissuaded as intended, and married Wilson anyway. And the people reelected Wilson anyway as well. Wilson involved Edith heavily in affairs of state, causing even more sad faces within his administration, and even included her on his trip to sign the armistice ending WWI. Then, crisscrossing the country trying to sell his idea for a League of Nations, the president worked himself to exhaustion and suffered a massive stroke. Wilson was confined to his bed and Edith, who was no more a fan of his staff than it was of her, became the gatekeeper to the president. She kept his condition secret not just from the public, but from the cabinet secretaries. When someone appeared with official business, she would take the paperwork in to the president and read it to him, or so she said. She returned with the president's "decision," and indecipherable annotations in the margins that some suspected Edith had scratched out herself. This went on for nearly a year and a half. Edith went to her grave steadfastly insisting that she never made decisions, save for what was important and what was not. But for the last third of Wilson's term, many historians agree America had a woman at the helm.

CHAPTER 6
THE POLITICS OF LEGISLATION

The production of sausage and legislation, so the saying goes, is not to be viewed by people with weak stomachs. Sniping, horse trading, and sleight of hand are par for the course. And sometimes the votes in Congress are only half the story. Modern politicians are sometimes accused of creating a baseless uproar, a red herring to take the public's attention off more problematic issues. The treaty that led to the acquisition of Alaska shows that this technique has deep roots. Russia had long been eager to divest of the far-flung region (later to be known as "Siberia's Siberia) in the 1850s, under the theory that America or Britain would eventually take it by force. But Britain felt that, in Canada, it had quite enough wilderness, and America had the brewing Civil War to deal with. It wasn't until the soon-to-be-impeached President Andrew Johnson needed a diversion from his domestic problems that the issue of Alaska was revisited. It worked initially, as pro- and anti-purchase forces chose up sides, and the treaty went to the Senate where it was approved by a single vote. But Johnson was eventually impeached by the House. The Senate declined to convict by the same one-vote margin, so in the end we kept a president and gained a state.

The Swedish government must approve the names of newborn children, under a law passed in 1982. The logic, people believe, is to prevent commoners from copying royalty, although the government cover story is that it protects the child against offensive names. The Swedish bureaucrats have allowed child names of "Google" and "Lego," but they have drawn the line at "Ikea" and "Allah," and they thwarted two parents who, in protest of the law, tried to name their child "Brfxxccxxmnpccclllmmnprxvclmnckssqlbb11116."

Queen Victoria was devastated by the loss of her husband, Prince Albert, in 1861. For the next 40 years of her life she dressed in black, and when she needed help with a particularly thorny legislative problem, she sought his help by trying to summon his spirit from beyond the grave.

In January 1803, Congress met in secret, emerging to say that the only thing it had done was pass a $2,500 expenditure "for the purpose of extending the external commerce of the United States." This measure, more commonly known as the Lewis and Clark expedition, was closely followed by the greatest expansion in American history, the Louisiana Purchase. Napoleon, who sold the Louisiana Territory to America, used the money for an arms buildup in anticipation of an invasion of Britain. The invasion never happened. Napoleon had few qualms about selling such a valuable piece of territory, figuring he could just reconquer it later. But that didn't happen either.

Legislative pay has always been a thorny issue, and politicians frequently run on pledges to turn down their salaries if elected— one of many promises they generally fail to live up to. In 1816, Congress raised its pay from $900 a year to $1,500. Largely because of this, two-thirds of House members were voted out of office in the ensuing election. Congress repealed the pay raise and the issue didn't come up again for another 4 decades.

> The framers of the Constitution had considered tying lawmakers' salaries to the price of wheat.

Western territorial legislatures drew the particular ire of Mark Twain, who mused "one of the first achievements of the legislature was to institute a ten-thousand-dollar agricultural fair to show off forty dollars' worth of pumpkins."

Constitutional amendments that failed to fly over the years include: making divorce illegal, capping incomes at $1 million, changing America's name to The United States of Earth, and replacing the residency with a Roman-style, three-member triumvirate.

Venice has a law against feeding pigeons; Singapore has a law against chewing gum in its subway. Eating isn't allowed in the Washington, D.C. subway.

Vermont's state pie is the apple pie. According to state law, a "good faith" effort must be made to serve a slice of apple pie with cold milk, ice cream, or a slice of cheese. State law specifies that the cheese be cheddar, and a minimum of a half-ounce.

Social Security legislation in 1935 was far less contentious than the Affordable Care Act. It passed 372 to 33 in the House, and 77 to 6 in the Senate.

Social Security, of a sort, got its start courtesy of the Civil War when Congress extended old-age pensions to veterans.

Social Security wasn't taxed until 1983 under President Ronald Reagan.

Congress has proposed a number of bills designed to "fix" Social Security. But Social Security still has some life left. The fund ended 2016 with $2.85 trillion in reserves and ran a surplus for the year. Reserves are expected to hold out, all things being equal, until 2034.

> Lawmakers designed Social Security to account for 40 percent of the retiree's pre-retirement income. But a third of Americans have no other income in retirement besides Social Security.

Despite 20 years of trying, Congress and the Justice Department have yet to unearth any significant episodes of voter fraud.

★

Two problems became evident after the Treaty of Paris ended the American Revolution. One, the new nation was heavily in debt and the Articles of Confederation, which pre-dated the Constitution, did not permit federal taxation. Second, even though Native Americans generally had sided with the British, many Indians felt the peace treaty did not apply to them, so when the government began selling off land in what is now the upper Midwest to pay its debts, several tribes were disinclined to take the sale of what they believed to be their land sitting down. Congress authorized a military force to enforce its policy. But early Congresses were notoriously cheap. Members authorized a regiment for only 6 months and at the same time voted to cut soldiers' pay. As a result, the American forces were much smaller than they needed to be and not in the best of spirits. The two sides met in battle in western Ohio on November 4th, 1791 with roughly equal numbers. The Battle of Little Bighorn is famously commemorated in American history as a terrible defeat, but it was nowhere near as bad as what became known as The Battle of a Thousand Slain. Of the nearly 1,000 American soldiers, only 24 emerged unscathed, for a casualty rate of 97 percent, the highest in American history. After this terrible defeat, Congress got back to work looking for every possible (inexpensive) way it could think of to enforce its will. The results were the Militia Acts of 1792 that conscripted every able-bodied white male (members of Congress themselves, of course, were exempt) between the ages of 18 and 45 in militias answerable to the President. Forget the right to bear arms, these militiamen were required to own muskets—along with a bayonet, two spare flints, a cartridge box, 24 bullets, and a knapsack. The Constitution would, 7 years later, reinforce this requirement with the familiar right to bear arms in the 2nd Amendment.

The Unlawful Games Act of 1541 required every Englishman between the ages of 17 and 60 to keep a longbow and regularly practice archery. The law was repealed in 1960.

Henry VIII, Mary I, and Elizabeth I regulated clothing styles through, among others, the 1562 Articles for the Execution of the Statutes of Apparel. This law prohibited anyone from appearing at the royal court wearing shirts with "outrageous double ruffs," or hose of "monstrous and outrageous greatness." These laws were for the most part repealed by James I.

The Madhouses Act of 1774 made it an offense in Britain to keep "more than one Lunatic" in the home without being a licensed asylum.

Since 1839, it's been illegal in England to be drunk in a bar. This might be an instance of Britain being ahead of its time, since prohibitions against selling liquor to people who have been over-served are becoming more common; but the Metropolitan Police Act of 1839 banned other types of fun as well, including flying a kite, playing annoying games, sledding in the streets, and for some reason "carrying a plank alongside a pavement." But the har-rumphing didn't stop there. The same statute made it illegal to sing profane songs in the street, to keep pigs in the front yard and to willfully and wantonly run away after knocking on someone's door. Rugs were not to be beaten in the street, but it was okay to beat doormats as long as it was prior to 8 a.m.

> A century before anyone had heard of DUI, it was illegal in England to drive drunk on a horse.

In 2012, North Carolina passed a law prohibiting state plan-ning agencies from acknowledging rising sea levels.

CHAPTER 7
THE POLITICS OF SEX

When President Bill Clinton wagged his finger and said, "I did not have sex with that woman, Miss Lewinsky," few people beyond his most ardent supporters took him at his word. By that time, it had been pretty well-established that "Slick Willy," as he was known among his not-so-ardent supporters, had something of a track record in that regard.

The #MeToo movement has changed things, perhaps, but the voting public has always been tolerant of sexual proclivities of its elected leaders, provided there are other things about the candidate to like. Indeed, there have often been double, even triple and quadruple standards when it comes to sex. Poor Jimmy Carter, a relatively unpopular president, got hooted off the stage not for any extramarital affair, but for simply admitting to *Playboy* magazine that "I've looked on a lot of women with lust. I've committed adultery in my heart many times."

★

By contrast, Jack Kennedy's lust expressed itself in organs other than his heart. But he got a pass from the public, which viewed him—somewhat positively, in fact—as a "ladies' man." In politics, a robust libido seems to only have been a detriment to men who expressly denied their robust libido. LBJ's nighttime forays to the bedchambers of female staffers ("Slide over darlin', it's your president") were laughed off because he didn't seem to mind his reputation as a hound dog.

For the sexual deniers, however (Trump being the exception), dalliances have inevitably resulted in the walk of shame, where the political perp trudges to the microphone—his wife, jaw clenched, stoically at his side—to confess that, come to think of it, he has been unfaithful after all. Unless, of course, women are to blame—as history shows, it's happened.

In 1155 BC, Pharaoh Ramses III of Egypt was murdered in a conspiracy among his wife Tiye, the royal harem, and other members of the court. A 12-judge panel was appointed to try the case, at which point the royal harem got into the act, partying with and seducing 3 members of the judiciary. In the end, the plot did not work out as intended. About 40 members of the court were executed; one of the 3 naughty judges was allowed to kill himself, the second had his nose and ears chopped off, and the third skated after turning the state's evidence.

> Clinton *et al.* might have done better in ancient Greece, where politicians would not have encountered the sexual hang-ups and expectations that we experience today. Men, who seldom married before the age of 30, favored wives for companionship, prostitutes for sex, and young boys for a combination of the two.

Still, sex could be used against a politician in certain circumstances. In 346 BC, the politician Aeschines attacked rival politician Timarchus on the grounds that he had as a young boy accepted money for sex. The theory under Attic law was that anyone who would sell sexual favors would also not hesitate to sell government favors. Aeschines himself was involved with a number of "beautiful boys," as the saying went, but of course that was okay because no money changed hands. The boys still received something of value in exchange for their favors, since it was assumed they would learn about politics, the military, and society from the older, wiser companion.

Pederasty was thought to promote democracy, because the love between a man and a boy would always be stronger than between a man and a tyrant. This came into play in 527 BC when the ruler Hipparchus tried to use his power to win the affections of a young boy, who was already in a relationship with an older man. Seeing no good ending, the two confronted Hipparchus at a festival and stabbed him to death. The pair were executed, but later a statue was erected to their memory and their willingness to stand up to a tyrant.

Scholars believe that Greek art depicting orgies might be a representation of actual events, but they also might be tongue-in-cheek commentaries on the dangers of over-imbibing.

Despite the wild stereotypes, Romans were more of what we have come to think of as traditional (and could be somewhat prudish) in their sexuality in comparison with the Greeks. But they did have their moments. When the emperor Tiberius found his standard methods of arousal failing him, he set up a theater and hired male and female prostitutes, along with "inventors of monstrous couplings so that, intertwining themselves and forming a triple chain they mutually prostituted themselves in front of him." If that didn't do the trick, it's hard to think anything would.

> **The widespread notion of Rome as one big drunken orgy was at least in part a myth perpetuated by early Christians engaged in spreading negative propaganda about the Romans.**

Which is not to say that Rome didn't have its moments. A nobleman named Decius Mundus during the reign of Tiberius seduced a married woman by putting on a dog head and pretending to be a god. The government priests who facilitated this subterfuge were executed, while Decius got off with just being exiled.

The Roman emperor Elagabalus assumed power at age 14 in 218 BC. By age 18 his sexual debauchery reached such heights that he was assassinated and replaced by his cousin.

Those who are unclear about whether or not it is a good idea to wear someone else's underpants should consider the case of Xia Ji, a married woman in China circa 600 BC who was carrying on with Duke Ling in the state of Chen and several of his ministers—all of whom found it funny, or sexy, or something, to wear her underwear. When Xia's son showed up one day, the officials began to joke around about which one of them the son most resembled, an insult the young man addressed by murdering the duke.

Under ruler Qin Shi Huang, the first emperor of China, the monarch's unsatisfied mother employed the services of a particularly well-endowed man to keep her happy. It was a good choice since the man's parlor trick was to bring in a wheel and roll it around the room using his penis as an axle. This talent didn't save him from execution when he was discovered.

The transition of Rome from a republic to an empire introduced government to the bedroom, where Rome's first Augustus laid down the law. Adultery, which in the past had largely been a family matter, was now outlawed by the state. Some have interpreted

this as a response to strong, elite women who were increasingly taking the initiative to choose their own lovers.

During the Roman Empire, boys entering manhood were enrolled
in the government census as a citizen, assigned to military service, and
shown the ropes, sexually speaking, by an older female prostitute.

> Under Roman law, a slave
> could not bring charges of
> rape against an aggressor,
> but the slave's owner could.

The state-sponsored Vestal Virgins took a vow of chastity, but
among the art objects under their watch was a sacred penis.

Not all scandals were legitimate scandals. In 1791, Andrew
Jackson married Rachel Donelson, who had escaped the clutches
of an alcoholic, abusive ex. Or, as it turned out, not quite ex,
because the divorce paperwork had not been properly processed.
The couple discovered the error and remarried in 1794. But by

that time, Jackson's political opponents, who were loyal to John Quincy Adams, had gotten wind of the situation, and accused him of living with a bigamist. Shortly after Jackson was elected president in 1828, Rachel collapsed due to what was said to be a nervous breakdown, and died. Jackson would forever blame his political enemies for her death.

James Henry Hammond of South Carolina was elected to the House of Representatives in 1835, but it is not the career he is known for. Beyond politics, he maintained a homosexual relationship with a college friend, sexually abused four of his teenage nieces, and maintained sexual relationships with female slaves, including a 12-year-old girl. When his seamy private life was made public, the people of South Carolina responded by electing him to the US Senate.

Warren G. Harding is sometimes regarded as the worst president in US history, but in his defense, he was busy with other things. In fact, the list of his affairs handily eclipses the list of his accomplishments. One of his belles, Nan Britton, wrote a tell-all book, claiming he had fathered her daughter when he was acting as US Senator. With the advent of genetic testing, her claims were confirmed in 2015.

In 1963, at the height of the Cold War, British Secretary of State for War John Profumo had a brief affair with a 19-year-old topless showgirl named Christine Keeler. It might not have amounted to much until it came to light that Keeler was also having an affair with a Russian intelligence officer. Pressure on the Conservative Party became so intense that both Profumo and Prime Minister Harold Macmillan resigned and the Conservatives lost the 1964 election. Stephen Ward, the English socialite who facilitated the liaisons, was charged with immorality, but killed himself while awaiting sentencing. It later came out that Stephen Ward was working for the British intelligence agency MI5, trying to use Keeler's charms to encourage the Russian officer to defect. The entry of the high-ranking Profumo into the seedy scene was an obvious complication.

Sexual affairs in Congress have of course been common enough, but no one grabbed the headlines like Wilbur Mills, an Arkansas Democrat who was once considered to be among the most powerful politicians in Washington. At 2 a.m. on October 9th, 1974 Mills was stopped by US Park Police, who found him to be drunk and suffering from facial injuries inflicted by his companion, a stripper who went by the stage name of Fanny Foxe with the nickname Argentine Firecracker. Foxe famously tried to escape by jumping into the Tidal Basin, and was subsequently taken to a local mental hospital for evaluation. One month later, Mills was reelected to Congress with 60 percent of the vote. Mills later joined AA and checked himself in for treatment of alcoholism, and Fanny Fox cashed in with a book and an upgrade in her moniker, from the Argentine Firecracker to the Tidal Basin Bombshell.

★

As one-liners from 1970s mistresses go, even the effervescent Fanny Foxe couldn't match Elizabeth Raye, who was on the payroll of a committee run by Ohio Congressional Democrat Wayne Hays as a secretary. Her real duties, however, were more bedroom than boardroom. When pressed, she admitted that "I can't type, I can't file, I can't even answer the phone." Instead, she was paid $14,000 a year to have sex with Hays.

> Hays resigned in 1976, which was perhaps something of a watershed year in that politicians caught in hanky panky prior to Hays generally held onto their jobs. Post-Hays, not so much.

In 1981, Rep. Thomas Evans, a Delaware Republican, went on a golf outing with lobbyist and Playboy bunny Paula Parkenson, who later explained that her lobbying technique that day had been "unusually tactile." Dan Quayle of Indiana, and future vice president of the United States, was on the golf outing as well, but his wife Marilyn said she had no concerns because everyone knew that her husband "would rather play golf than have sex any day."

Tactile or not, Parkenson was effective. All three members voted against the crop-insurance bill she did not want them to support.

The summer of 1983 was particularly steamy for congressmen Dan Crane and Gerry Studds, who were censured on the same July day, the former for having sex with a female page, the latter for having a relationship with a young male staffer. Leading the call for full expulsion from the House was Newt Gingrich, who a decade later would have an affair with a staffer 20 years younger than he. Following their respective embarrassments, Studds was reelected, Crane was not. Gingrich, meanwhile, when asked about his infidelities in 2011, blamed patriotism. "There's no question at times in my life, partially driven by how passionately I felt about this country, that I worked too hard and things happened in my life that were not appropriate," he told David Brody of the Christian Broadcasting Network.

Quaint as it might seem, the 1980s was a time when even the suggestion of an extramarital affair could kill the candidacy of a presidential aspirant. Ask Gary Hart, who was relentlessly dogged by the press over questions of his womanizing. In frustration he told the media, "Follow me around. I don't care. I'm serious. If anybody wants to put a tail on me, go ahead. They'll be very bored." That proved to be an unwise challenge. Hart eventually dropped out of the race after being photographed on a boat with a young woman named Donna Rice. The name of the boat was equally unfortunate: *Monkey Business*. After firing back at the press, whom he called "animals," during his withdrawal press conference, Hart received a note of condolence from someone who felt he knew a thing or two about perceived media harassment—Richard Nixon.

Ernie Konnyu, a California representative, asked a female staffer to remove her nametag. The reason? Because it was drawing too much attention to her breasts. This caused a few people to wince, but when afforded the opportunity to explain himself, he replied, "She is not exactly heavily stacked, okay?" His response did little to clear the air. Republicans, who in those days kept their own house, found a more suitable candidate who knocked off Konnyu in the 1987 primary.

Senator Brock Adams was publicly accused by the daughter of longtime friends that he had drugged and sexually assaulted her at his home. Adams, a Washington State Democrat, denied the accusations, saying they were merely discussing job opportunities, but 8 other women came forward describing a pattern over 20 years of drug-aided rape. The only consequence for Adams, as demanded by the party, was to drop his reelection campaign in order to ensure the seat would stay safely in Democratic hands.

In 1989, an Ohio mother confronted Rep. Donald "Buz" Lukens, a conservative activist, on videotape of paying to have sex with her 13-year-old daughter. A court found Lukens guilty of contributing to the delinquency of a minor, and was sentenced to a month in jail. Lukens found no reason, however, to think this was cause for resigning his House seat, and chugged right along until he was caught groping an elevator operator in the US Capitol.

In 1991, the married Virginia Sen. Chuck Robb expected the voting public to believe that he had spent the night in a hotel room with Tai Collins, a former Miss Virginia, and all that took place was a backrub. The public may or may not have believed him, but they did reelect him. It helped that his opponent was Ollie North, who during the Iran-Contra scandal stood accused of illegally putting weapons into the hands of a group of Latin American rebels. Collins went on to pose nude in *Playboy* magazine.

★

When Bill Clinton's dalliance with Monica Lewinsky came to light, congressional Republicans appeared before the TV cameras en masse to talk about how disgusting it was to carry on with this sort of sexual shenanigans. Then the other shoe (or more accurately, pants) began to drop, as it turned out the president was not the only one in government doing what he ought not.

> "As he was spearheading the Clinton impeachment hearings, Henry Hyde copped to a previous extramarital affair with a married mother of 3, which he said was different from Clinton's because it was due to a "youthful indiscretion.""

Helen Chenoweth-Hage, who was convinced the government was landing black helicopters on Idaho ranches at the behest of the Environmental Protection Agency, was among the first to call for Clinton's resignation. When it was revealed that she had been involved for years with a married rancher prior to assuming office, she said her circumstance was different from Clinton's because she had "asked for God's forgiveness," a favor she assured her constituency that the Almighty had been all too happy to grant her.

Florida Congressman Mark Foley said of Bill Clinton, "It's vile. It's sadder than anything else, to see someone with such potential throw it all down the drain because of a sexual addiction." Eight years later Foley resigned for engaging in cybersex with teenage boys.

Sen. Pete Domenici voted for impeachment, although it was later revealed that he too had fathered a child out of wedlock, the mother being the daughter of fellow Senator Paul Laxalt. And of course, there was Gingrich, whose own infidelities as he pursued Clinton's impeachment were the least convenient.

In the 1950s and 60s, the Canadian government was so paranoid about homosexuality that it employed a "Fruit Machine" that could supposedly detect gay men. The subjects were shown homoerotic films and the machine would measure pupil dilation. The idea was that pupils would widen with excitement. Before the project was abandoned later in the decade, many men had lost their jobs based on scientifically dubious data.

Unimpressed by stories of President Kennedy's sexual conquests, Vice President Lyndon Johnson would drawl that he's had more women by accident than Kennedy ever had on purpose.

CHAPTER 8
THE POLITICS OF VIOLENCE

For all our hot-button political issues today, none could compare to the Kansas-Nebraska Act, which was intended to facilitate a Midwestern Railroad, but, as with everything in the mid-1800s, slavery reared its ugly head. The issue became a referendum on the 1820 Missouri Compromise, which was seen by southerners as an unacceptable brake on the expansion of slavery. On June 20th, 1854 violence erupted on the floor of the US House when two Tennessee representatives blew their stacks. The protagonists were William Churchwell and William Cullom, who had previously been friends until Churchwell accused Cullom and Tennessee Sen. John Bell of defending the Missouri Compromise. In the eyes of a southerner there was no greater sin.

Bell responded by putting down Churchwell's character by saying that anyone within earshot of Churchwell had to consider the source. Churchwell said Bell was making a personal attack instead of relying on the facts. Cullom chimed in that Churchwell's facts weren't facts at all, but merely fake news. And that's where things stood on June 20th, when Churchwell accused Cullom of tampering with the Congressional Record to smear his reputation. For Cullom, this was the last straw. He leaped across his desk at his fellow Tennessean, who responded by reaching for a gun. Bloodshed was averted when another congressman grabbed the weapon before Churchwell could fire. The next day the two men apologized, and neither was in any way punished. *The New York Times* was not satisfied with this outcome however, calling it a disgrace and calling for a roll call vote so citizens would know "who among the members are in favor of converting the Representative Chamber into a shooting-gallery, and who are not."

Representative Preston Brooks, a South Carolina hothead, introduced two resolutions in response to congressional violence: one to expel any member who might brandish a firearm in the future, the other to order the Sergeant at Arms to build a gun rack in the rotunda where members could park their pieces before entering the chamber.

There was, of course, great irony in Brooks, of all people, representing himself as a great peacemaker. Two years later he almost beat to death Sen. Charles Sumner on the floor of the Senate with the head of his cane. As Sumner lay bleeding, no one thought to stop Brooks as he calmly walked from the Senate floor.

> Brooks became an immediate hero in the South. He resigned his House seat, but was later reelected. He did not live to see the Civil War, dying shortly after his reelection at age 37. Sumner slowly recovered and went on to serve another 18 years in the Senate.

If anything is to be learned from congressional violence, it is this: Do not try to settle your arguments with tobacco juice. In the winter of 1798, Representatives Roger Griswold and Matthew Lyon got into it over foreign policy, a debate Lyon tried to win with a well-placed hock from his wad of tobacco. Griswold went after Lyon with his cane, and Lyon defended himself with a set of fireplace tongs. Deciding that boys will be boys, the House voted 21–73 against expulsion.

★

Everyone, especially the newspapers, had a good laugh over Griswold and Lyon, but a dispute in the Capitol in 1838 ended tragically. Jonathan Cilley of Maine was killed by Representative William Graves of Kentucky, just outside the District of Columbia. The two men had no particular grudge against each other, but as these things went, hostilities rapidly escalated when a Southerner conceived of a slight against his honor. In this case, the slight seemed particularly slight. Graves had been given a poison-pen letter written by a newspaper editor, in hopes that he would deliver it to Cilley. When Cilley refused to accept it, Graves felt his honor had been dinged.

A would-be-assassin tried to kill Andrew Jackson, but when the gun misfired, the 67-year-old president beat the daylights out of the man with his walking stick.

In 221 BC, China was unified under the first (he invented the word) "emperor," Qin Shi Hungdi. As one might expect for that place and time, he did not do so through peaceful negotiations.

Still, his reputation for violence might be overstated since it was a subsequent, and hostile, dynasty that wrote his history. If it's true though, Qin went to outlandish extremes to control thought. According to Records of the Grand Historian, Qin's chancellor Li Si dictated: "Anyone who dares to discuss the *Shi Jing* [a book of Confucian poetry] or the *Classic of History* [a book of political philosophy] shall be publicly executed. Anyone who uses history to criticize the present shall have his family executed. Any official who sees the violations but fails to report them is equally guilty. Anyone who has failed to burn the books after thirty days of this announcement shall be subjected to tattooing and be sent to build the Great Wall." Confucian scholars fared little better. Qin was accused, perhaps with some hyperbole, of burying at least 460 scholars alive after he became dissatisfied with the work of a couple of alchemists.

Those who believe they have complex family issues would have a hard time matching Qin. His mother maintained an affair with a wealthy chancellor who skipped town when he felt the affair was about to be exposed. In his absence, he wanted to keep his mistress happy, so he appointed a man named Lao Ai to perform his duties (tough job, but someone has to do it). To avoid suspicion, he brought Lao Ai into the court in the role of a eunuch. As eunuchs go, of course, he was a failure, because the couple wound up having two sons together. Unfortunately, Lao Ai let his station go to his head. At a dinner party he was apparently overserved, and began to boast that he was effectively Qin's stepfather. This had consequences that led to a large price being placed on Lao Ai's head.

At this point—in for a penny, in for a pound—Lao Ai led an open rebellion against Qin. But he turned out to be no better a soldier than he was a eunuch. He was captured and torn into five pieces by horse-drawn carriages. His supporters were beheaded, his family executed, the two sons he had with the queen were killed, and the queen herself spent the rest of her life under lock and key. The chancellor, who had started the whole mess, saw the handwriting on the wall and drank poison.

> Attila the Hun, aka the Scourge of God, died on his wedding night in 453 after choking on his own blood. Possibly this was from overindulging, or possibly from something more. Those who buried him were executed so the location of his grave would never be known.

Oliver Cromwell might have wished he had thought of the hidden-grave trick. Cromwell led and won the English Civil War that overturned the monarchy and led to the execution of the king, Charles I. Cromwell died of a urinary infection in 1658 at the age of 59. He was buried with great fanfare at Westminster Abbey, but his rest did not prove to be as eternal as he might have hoped. After Cromwell's death his government faltered and by 1660, the monarchists were back in power under Charles II. Cromwell's body was pulled from the Abbey floor and his head was chopped off. The body was hanged in chains, before being thrown into a pit. His head, however, enjoyed quite a journey. It was sold a number of times, and occasionally placed on public display. In 1960 it was buried beneath the floor of a college chapel in Cambridge. But by then the lesson had been learned; its exact location was not disclosed.

Cromwell justified the execution of Charles I through his interpretation of the Bible, specifically the book of Numbers: "The land cannot be cleansed of the blood that is shed therein, but by the blood of him that shed it." This was something of a difficult case to make, since kings derived their authority—which in theory was not to be questioned—from God.

The abuse of Cromwell's corpse was not the worst on record. That honor might go to Pope Formosus, predecessor to Pope Stephen VI. Stephen felt he had been slighted by Formosus, so he had the remains of his adversary dug up and propped up on a throne and placed on trial. Being unable to defend himself due to an advancing state of decay, a deacon was appointed to speak for him as an appalled "jury" of clergy. The cadaver was found guilty, stripped of honors, relieved of three of his fingers, and reburied. That being, on reflection, too good for him, he was dug up again and thrown in a river. But so ghastly was the whole affair that the church decided to make an exception to this infallibility business. Stephen was imprisoned in 897 and later strangled.

Genghis Khan was born holding a blood clot in his right hand. His mother had been kidnapped and forced into marriage. His father was poisoned when the boy was 9. It would not take a child psychologist to predict how this was going to turn out. He became one of the bloodiest rulers in world history, uniting the notoriously divided Mongols and setting in motion what would become the largest contiguous empire in world history.

Setting the tone for future battles was the conquest of the Khwarezmid Empire in present day Iran and Afghanistan. Genghis Kahn was initially more interested in peaceful trade than war, but a provincial governor made the mistake of detaining a Mongol trading caravan and accusing its members of being spies. The Khan sent three emissaries to the Shah. The Shah had two of them shaved and decapitated the third, sending the two survivors back to Genghis Kahn with instructions to present the Mongol leader with the third envoy's head. The Khan responded by essentially wiping the Khwarezmid Empire from the map.

In perhaps one of the most brutal aftermaths, when the Mongols conquered the wealthy trading city of Urgench, each of 50,000 Mongol soldiers was, the story went, ordered to murder 24 civilians, for a total of 1.2 million people.

The total numbers slaughtered by the Mongols are difficult to know, since among their tactics to instill fear among their enemies was the exaggeration of past bloodbaths. The Mongols spared and employed the useful artisans of a city, but massacred wholesale the aristocrats and elite.

For a tyrant, Genghis Khan was remarkable for his tolerance in some areas, being one of the first world rulers to allow freedom of religion. He also established the first international postal system.

Genghis Khan's last ruling descendent was deposed in 1920.

Genghis and Attila might have gotten more press, but no one was bloodier than Timur, the self-styled Sword of Islam. Timur, born in 1336, was the bridge between the great conquerors of Eurasian Steppe and more structured dynasties to come. He might also have been the bloodiest fighter in history. His wars were said to have cost the lives of 17 million people, or about 5 percent of the world's population. With his captives he was particularly creative. He would build mountains out of their skulls, and in a least one instance cemented 2,000 of them into a pyramid while they were still alive.

When the city of Isfahan balked at paying Timur's taxes, he massacred up to 200,000 of its citizens.

In an attack on Delhi, Timur's troops faced war elephants, of which it soon became apparent they were much afraid. Timur's answer was to load his camels with straw and wood, prod them toward the enemy, and set them afire. Timur had a reputation for intelligence, and he knew that elephants could be easily spooked—as would happen when they saw a stampede of camels shrieking in pain headed their way. The elephants turned and trampled their own troops.

★

After capturing Baghdad, Timur ordered each soldier to return with 2 severed heads to show him. There were more soldiers than there were citizens, and when they ran out of citizens, they started beheading prisoners of war. When these were gone, so terrified were the men of Timur, that they started beheading their own wives.

> Timur, or Tamerlane, was somewhat popular in Europe, where he was seen as a counterbalance to the Ottomans, and he remains a heroic figure in much of his home territory on the steppes today.

Timur's body was exhumed by the Soviets and examined by an anthropologist. On the inside of his casket, legend has it, was the transcription: "Whomsoever opens my tomb shall unleash an invader more terrible than I." Three days later Hitler invaded the Soviet Union. Timur was reburied a year later in a full Islamic ceremony, just before the Soviets defeated the Germans in the Battle of Stalingrad.

With a name like Ivan the Terrible, Ivan must have been, well, terrible, and in this sense the Russian tsar who ruled in the 1500s does not disappoint. In putting down a suspected insurgency (the somewhat unstable Ivan suspected most all nobles of insurgency) in the thriving city of Novgorod in 1570, his army roasted the men to death before hot coals, and tied women and children to sleighs and dragged them through the streets before throwing them into the icy river, where patrolling soldiers in boats poked those who surfaced back beneath the water with pikes. He next marched on the city of Pskov, but for some reason had a change of heart. According to legend, of which there are several versions, Ivan was greeted at the gates by Nikola Salos, a religious zealot whose mental state was not all that far removed from the tsar's. Salos swore at Ivan and shoved a piece of raw meat in his face suggesting that Ivan take a bite since he found "the meat of Christians" to be so appealing. Ivan spared the city. Not spared was Ivan's own son. The tsar had just beaten his pregnant daughter-in-law—possibly causing a miscarriage—for wearing immodest clothing when his son interceded. Ivan took a swing at his son with a pointed staff and connected, killing him with the blow.

> "Ivan was a talented poet and composer. In 1988, some of his writings were put to music and released in honor of Christianity's millennium in Russian history."

In a nation with a history of terror, one of the more tragically bizarre episodes in Russia was the Holodomor, or death by starvation in Ukraine during the years 1932 and 1933. The famine itself was no surprise, having been predicted in the grain-producing regions since 1930, but perhaps fearing a Ukrainian independence movement, Joseph Stalin greatly exacerbated the effects. This "man-made famine" was brought on by Soviet policy, in which farmers were forced to turn their land over to the state and grow crops other than grain, such as cotton. When grain production plummeted, the Soviets implemented an ineffectual rationing program, and blamed the farmers by showing urban workers movies depicting people in the country as counterrevolutionaries who were trying to sabotage the "bright future" of communism. By the time it was over, between 3.3 million and 7.5 million people starved. It's believed that enough grain existed to feed the population had it been distributed properly, but much of it was taken away by the state for export. Offers of food relief from other nations were rejected. Many people were forced to feed on the bodies of the dead, a practice that was frowned upon by the state. About 2,500 people were convicted of cannibalism during the Holodomor.

In Cambodia, the Khmer Rouge killed at least 1.4 million of its own people between 1975 and 1979. Under Pol Pot, the government killed those with connections to the previous regime, and those in contact with foreigners, intellectuals, professionals, and ethnic minorities. So many were killed that the government could not afford ammunition and had to resort to sharpened bamboo stakes. Perceived enemies of the state were taken away for "reeducation" with the promise of forgiveness and a new start. They were subsequently slaughtered and thrown in mass graves. Their children were killed as well, to avoid the possibility that they might grow up and seek revenge for their parents' killings.

The purges of Stalin, which killed tens of millions of people, are legendary, but in 1950 Korea it was the communists who were massacred. The Bodo League massacre during the Korean War killed up to 200,000 people, a share of whom had no idea what a communist even was. The Bodo League was another reeducation effort, which was more interested in killing than reforming. Communists were enrolled in the program but so were non-communists in order for bureaucrats to meet their government quotas. One "communist" who was executed, according to an American witness, was a girl of about 12 years old. Despite American and British witnesses, the Bodo League Massacre largely remained a secret until the 1990s. Gen. Douglas McArthur referred to it as an "internal matter." A South Korean officer brushed off the killings, saying, "there was no time for trials."

Genocides have commenced on American shores as well. During the Gold Rush, up to 16,000 (some estimates are much higher) California Native Americans were killed, either randomly or by non-native death squads. This extermination of natives was a matter of government policy. California armed militias were encouraged to exterminate Native Americans who were considered to be a threat to the security of the newly discovered gold mines. To kill 16,000 people the government spent $53 million in today's dollars. Rather than punish the murderers, local governments rewarded them financially, especially if they returned from their killing sprees with the victims' horses. Under California law, white settlers could take Native American children. They could also arrest Native Americans for minor violations such as loitering and force them to work off their fines, effectively making them into slaves.

Americans got the short end of the stick in another round of state-sponsored terrorism, this at the hands of the Barbary Pirates off the African coast in the 18th century. For pirates, they were pretty well organized, even having an ambassador who met with the likes of Thomas Jefferson and Ben Franklin. African Muslim states backed the pirates, often encouraging them to operate, for a slice of the loot. The pirates considered themselves to be firm but fair, only chopping up their victims or hanging them from meat hooks if they resisted. Otherwise, they were content to allow ships to pass—for a well-established price. In another non-piratey move, these pirates would even enter into treaties with other nations, essentially codifying their blackmail.

When Somali pirates captured a United States merchant ship in 2009, the Navy sent to the rescue a destroyer, the USS Bainbridge, named after Commodore William Bainbridge who had embarrassingly lost a ship to the Tripoli pirates in 1803.

After the Vietnam War was over, another 50,000 Vietnamese died from stepping on buried mines and bombs.

CHAPTER 9
DIRTY POLITICAL TRICKS

There is nothing more American in American politics than the put-down and the political dirty trick. It is even older than the Republic itself, and early on, one of the go-to dirty tricks were accusations of cross dressing. If you wanted to stick it to your opponent you would say that he, in Monty Python parlance, "puts on women's clothing and hangs around in bars."

One of the first to be so accused was Edward Hyde, 3rd Earl of Clarendon aka the Viscount Cornbury. After bolting the Catholics of King James and siding with the protestant William III of Orange, the earl was rewarded with the governorship of New York in 1701. By 1706, he was wearing out his welcome with the colonists, as all royal governors tended to do. He was accused of embezzlement, fraud, bribery, and so forth. But since all royal governors were accused of this, his opponents needed something more attention grabbing, and what better than to paint him as "a degenerate and pervert who is said to have spent half of his time dressed in women's clothes."?

Some reported doing business with the governor as he was wearing women's dress, and seeing him dolled up as he sat in the window of the governor's mansion. Unlike Jefferson, as time passed, the story grew stronger, rather than fading into doubt. Viscount Cornbury was quoted as saying that since he represented Queen Anne, it was only proper that he adopt feminine dress. Today—no one knows. But there is no doubt that, true or not, his detractors found an issue that would stick.

An 18th century portrait hanging in the New York Historical Society of a heavy-jawed individual in a tiara and shimmering blue gown is thought by some to be Lord Cornbury. So, was his cross-dressing a fact or dirty put-down? We'll likely never know.

Political reporter and fearless Scot who had been run out of the British Isles for his political attacks, James T. Callender picked right back up in America where he had left off, his first two targets being the American Constitution and General George Washington. Mr. Callender did not believe in starting small and working his way up. The Constitution, he believed, was a sham because it failed to accurately reflect the will of the people. He thought Washington serendipitously promoted himself as an idol, and called his behavior "debauched."

Because of his attacks on the Federalists, Callendar was initially favored by Jefferson, who subsidized his writings and got him a job on a Republican newspaper. But Callender couldn't behave. He reported on an affair of Alexander Hamilton with a married woman, and eventually ran afoul of the new Sedition Act and was jailed. For his trouble, he expected a plumb appointment from Jefferson, one that was not forthcoming due to Jefferson's conclusion that the muckraker was too hot to handle. This caused Callender to turn his caustic pen on his former ally.

In September 1802, Callender wrote in a Richmond newspaper that President Thomas Jefferson had for many years, "kept, as his concubine, one of his own slaves" who went by the name of Sally, and that Jefferson had "several children" by her.

The Federalists, of course, ate up Callender's accusations against Jefferson with a spoon. His defenders wrote it off as fake news. Through the nation's history, the story of Jefferson and Sally Hemings was considered to be one of the earliest examples of dirty politics in America, perpetuated by that dirtiest of hacks, a journalist (with Callender it was somewhat a case of guilty as charged; his demise came when he got falling-down drunk and drowned in the James River). But, as we know now, Callender was right. According to the Thomas Jefferson Foundation, "Thomas Jefferson fathered at least six of Sally Heming's children. Four survived to adulthood and are mentioned in Jefferson's plantation records: Beverly, Harriet, Madison, and Eston Hemings. Sally Hemings worked for two and a half years (1787–89) in Paris as a domestic servant and maid in Jefferson's household. While in Paris, where she was free, she negotiated with Jefferson to return to enslavement at Monticello in exchange for "extraordinary privileges" for herself and freedom for her unborn children."

"Some of his detractors believed Jefferson to be "too French" in his habits to be a true American patriot.

Martin Van Buren might have been the first "metrosexual" president, which might be acceptable in the 21st century, but was not a thing one wanted to be associated with in the hard fighting, hard-drinking, men-are-men days of the mid-1800s. Rep. Charles Ogle took the floor in Congress and accused the president of pampering himself with Corinthian Oil of Cream and Extract of Eglantine, and in some circles, Van Buren was rumored to enjoy wearing a corset.

Ogle, a Pennsylvanian who won election on an anti-Mason platform, said the president was a fussy dandy "strutting by the hour before golden-framed mirrors nine feet high and four feet and a half wide in a palace as splendid as that of the Caesars and as richly adorned as the proudest Asiatic mansion." He ate with gold cutlery and into finger cups he would dip his "pretty tapering soft lily-white fingers." Charles Ogle's speech, which became known as the "Gold Spoon Oration," lasted for 3 days. Van Buren, in response, issued a weak statement certifying that he did not eat with gold utensils. The speech was credited with helping into office William Henry Harrison, who was in fact a Virginia aristocrat, but whose opponents categorized as a cabin-dwelling cider swiller. Contrasting himself with Van Buren, Harrison adopted this gig, effectively winning the presidency by characterizing himself as being a lout.

Martin Van Buren was the only president to speak English as a second language. As a child he spoke Dutch.

> Because of an economic depression
> during his presidency, Van Buren
> became known as Van Ruin.

Name-calling and accusations of dubious foundation were common in early America, although they tended to be more lyrical and poetic. The best remembered, perhaps came during the 1884 race between presidential contenders Grover Cleveland for the Democrats and Republican James G. Blaine, whose name, bad news for him, happened to rhyme with his home state. Cleveland meanwhile, despite his supporters' moniker of "Grover the Good," was accused of fathering a child out of wedlock.

Cleveland supporters heckled his opponent with cries of:
Blaine, Blaine James G. Blaine,
Continental liar from the state of Maine.

Blaine's sympathizers responded with a refrain of:
Ma, Ma, Where's my pa?

After the election, in which Cleveland was victorious, his sup-porters adopted the ditty for themselves, adding a line:

Ma, Ma, Where's my pa?
Gone to the White House, ha, ha, ha.

So there.

Even Republicans weren't sold on Blaine, largely due to allega-tions of corruption. Many wanted to draft Civil War Gen. William T. Sherman, who presumably would have found rough sledding in the American South. Sherman is the original political saw. "If drafted, I will not run; if nominated, I will not accept; if elected, I will not serve."

Blaine remains the only presidential candidate from Maine.

The accusations of corruption continued to dog Blaine in the campaign, as a sheaf of letters discovered by bookkeeper James Mulligan revealed Congressman Blaine had been knee-deep in vote-selling and influence peddling. He had taken $1.5 million in today's dollars to funnel a federal land grant to the Little Rock and Fort Smith Railroad. One of the pieces of correspondence bore the postscript, "Burn this letter," advice Blaine probably wished had been followed. Blaine's primary stumble, however, didn't involve corruption, it involved a throwaway line in a speech by the Rev. Samuel Burchard at a gathering of Republican protestant preachers. Burchard took a swipe at the Catholics, saying "We are Republicans, and don't propose to leave our party and identify with the party whose antecedents have been rum, Romanism, and Rebellion." Blaine was in attendance, but seemed not to have taken notice of the slur, or at least seen anything untoward about it. Neither, apparently did the assembled newspaper reporters. But political operatives monitored campaign events in those days, much as operatives today keep tabs on their opponents' social media feeds. Sure enough, a Cleveland man was in the audience, and soon Burchard's remarks were well publicized in Catholic circles, and Blaine's silence amounted to complicity, much like a modern-day retweet.

> "Burn this letter!" became a popular, derisive chant used against Blaine, much in the way "Lock her up!" was used against Hillary Clinton.

The 1884 elections included candidates from several other special interest parties, including those opposed to alcohol and monopolies, and in favor of women's rights. The Equal Rights Party nominated Washington, D.C. attorney Belva Ann Lockwood, even though most of the women who would be inclined to vote for her could not legally do so. Even Lockwood herself could not vote. No matter, she said. "I cannot vote, but I can be voted for."

It was the Prohibition Party, however, that might have had the most effect on the race. Prohibitionists tended to be Republicans, and Blaine worried that the Prohibitionists might siphon votes away from his campaign. His people tried to get the Prohibition candidate John St. John to drop out of the race, and when he refused, they launched a mud-smearing campaign against him. An infuriated St. John redoubled his efforts in New York, which ultimately Blaine lost by scarcely more than 1,000 votes. Winning New York would have won Blaine the election.

Grover Cleveland's decency was compared favorably to George Washington, perhaps the first and last American presidential candidate whose reputed goodness went largely, but not entirely, unchallenged.

George Washington lived by 110 "rules of civility" that he transcribed before he reached the age of 16. Some of these he would translate into his political life, or try to, but flea flicking aside, Washington had trouble living up to his own standards, as anyone would. Shortly after his compilation of character, Lord Fairfax wrote to Mary Ball Washington in 1748. "I wish I could say that he governs his temper, He is subject to attacks of anger on provocation, sometimes without just cause."

Tobias Lear, George Washington's secretary, is quoted as saying that "few sounds on Earth could compare with that of George Washington swearing a blue streak."

> History records that both Washington and Jefferson were known to throw their hats on the ground and stomp on them.

Other presidents famous for a bad temper include Harry Truman who, after his daughter's singing panned in *Washington Post*, wrote music critic Paul Hume in 1950 with the put-down, "It seems to me that you are a frustrated old man who wishes he could have been successful. Someday I hope to meet you. When that happens, you'll need a new nose, a lot of beefsteak for black eyes, and perhaps a supporter below!"

Washington battled his temper as well as the British. He publicly humiliated (against his own coda of civility) officers Adam Stephen and Charles Lee (both of whom deserved it), his temper erupting in the field and making quite an impression on the men in the ranks. For both of his targets, the feelings of antipathy were mutual. Stephen's primary adversary might have been the bottle— he had once gotten drunk and wound up attacking his own side— but George Washington was a close second. Stephen was a George Washington wannabe, seeking to be a wealthy and esteemed mover and shaker, but at every juncture in his career Washington had always been one business deal or promotion or land transaction ahead of him. It was military jealousy that had soured Gen. Lee on the Father of our Country, essentially because Lee wanted Father status for himself. Or at least leadership of the Continental Army, which he felt Washington was unfit to lead. Lee wrote to another Revolutionary ne'er-do-well Horatio Gates with the slam, "a certain great man is most damnably deficient . . . unless something we do not expect turns up, we are lost."

After the war, Gates, Lee, and Stephen all settled in the same area of what is now West Virginia, where they would get together and toast their various misfortunes.

Better men than the Lee-Stephen-Gates triumvirate savaged George Washington. 7 years after Washington's death, a crusty old John Adams wrote of what he called Washington's "ten talents,": "Washington was a Virginian. This is equivalent to five Talents. Virginian Geese are all Swans. Not a Bearne in Scotland is more national, not a Lad upon the High Lands is more clannish, than every Virginian I have ever known. They trumpet one another with the most pompous and mendacious Panegyricks. The Phyladelphians and New Yorkers who are local and partial enough to themselves are meek and modest in Comparison with Virginian Old Dominionisms. Washington of course was extolled without bounds."

Washington's stated virtues could be seen by others as vice. What he felt was proper decorum could be interpreted as coldness and pomposity. Wrote Thomas Paine: "It is laughable to hear Mr. Washington talk of his sympathetic feelings, who has always been remarked, even among his friends, for not having any." To Paine, Washington's morality walked a fine line: "The character which Mr. Washington has attempted to act in the world is a sort of nondescribable, chameleon-colored thing called prudence. It is, in many cases, a substitute for principle, and is so nearly allied to hypocrisy that it easily slides into it."

★

Presidential candidate Richard Nixon sabotaged peace talks between North and South Vietnam in 1968 by having an aide tell the South Vietnamese they would get a better deal once Nixon was elected. A plank in Nixon's platform called for an end to the war, and if it ended before the election—as it appeared was about to happen—Nixon feared he would lose a valuable campaign edge. Acting on Nixon's message, the South walked out of the peace talks in Paris, and another 22,000 Americans died before the war actually ended in 1973. President Lyndon Johnson knew of Nixon's interference, because he had bugged the South Vietnamese ambassador. But he didn't let on, because he did not believe Nixon could win—and he didn't want to admit to having bugged a foreign dignitary.

Joe Kennedy was a Nazi sympathizer and anti-Semite who supported Joe McCarthy. Even for the time, these views were out of step enough to deep-six his own political ambitions, leading him to promote his sons for office. He had plenty of money with which to lubricate the wheels of democracy, a fortune that was dubiously obtained. He played the market engaging in stock shorting, spreading rumors to drive stock prices up or down, and insider trading—all of which were, technically, legal. President Franklin D. Roosevelt in 1934 appointed Joe Kennedy head of the Securities and Exchange Commission on the grounds that "it takes a crook to catch a crook." Sure enough, Kennedy proceeded to outlaw all the shenanigans that had made him rich.

In his 1945 congressional race, Jack Kennedy faced several challengers, including Joe Russo. His dad allegedly found another

Joe Russo, a janitor, and paid him to run with the idea that confused voters would split their votes between the two Russos. If true,
it was money poorly spent, as neither Russo was a factor in the race.

JFK, aware of his father's reputation, once joked that he'd just
opened one of his father's letters which said. "Dear Jack, don't buy
one more vote than is necessary; I'll be damned if I'm going to pay
for a landslide."

> Jack's politics were very different from his dad's, and Joe reportedly intimated to Richard Nixon in 1960 that if it weren't for family ties, he'd be a Nixon man.

Richard "Tricky Dick" Nixon, of course, was hard to outgun
when it came to political shenanigans. In 1972, a member of his
White House team mailed a forged letter to the *Manchester Union-
Leader* newspaper, ostensibly from a person who had talked to
Democratic frontrunner Edmund Muskie in Florida and asked

how he could understand the needs of African Americans, seeing as how Muskie's home state of Maine had so few. The letter related that a Muskie staffer said that Maine didn't have blacks, but it did have Canucks, a response that purportedly drew a chuckle from Muskie. The exchange was designed to be a slur against voters with French Canadian connections, and came just 2 weeks before the New Hampshire primary. The next day in a snowstorm, Muskie gave a speech outside the newspaper offices, calling out its publisher, William Loeb, for taking the bait, and also for impugning the character of the candidate's wife. Muskie's voice cracked with emotion, which he said was from anger, but what reports indicated was despair. This called into question his emotional suitability and his candidacy imploded. Reporters, detecting moisture on Muskie's face, said he was weeping, and his oratory became known as "the crying speech." Muskie said the "tears" were in fact melting snowflakes. Back in the days when there was no greater kiss of death for a candidate than to be tied to the Soviet Union, Loeb referred to the Democrat as "Moscow Muskie." Muskie actually won the New Hampshire primary, but by less of a margin than was expected, and his candidacy was quickly overtaken by George McGovern. The Nixon hatchet men responsible for the letter went by the name of Committee for the Re-Election of the President, or CREEP.

Nineteen-year-old Republican Yvonne Dean-Bailey was elected to the New Hampshire legislature on May 19th, 2015, despite an aide to her Democratic opponent, Maureen Mann, emailing reporters to inform them that Dean-Bailey would be dropping out of the race to focus on her schoolwork. Aide Carl Gibson's trick was quickly discovered, and he later admitted that he probably had one too many beers before sending the press release.

CHAPTER 10
WOMEN IN POLITICS

Women have been involved in politics since the beginning of the written record, but their contributions have often been overlooked in the public record, most likely because the public record was written by men. But even when not specifically in power, women have had a way of getting their points across.

In ancient Rome, of course, there was no shortage of women who viewed romance and power as notes of the same tune. One of the most fascinating was Julia Agrippina, who was the common denominator among a number of controversial Roman rulers. The sister of Caligua, wife of Claudius, and mother of Nero, she was suspected of poisoning inconvenient family members right and left, before manipulating her son into power. A chip off the old block, Nero murdered her before she had a chance to murder him.

The first woman to speak on the floor of the House of Representatives chamber was Dorothy Ripley, who preached there in 1806. Because there were no sizable meeting halls in Washington, D.C. through the first half of the 19th century, the Capitol building often did double duty as a church.

The House of Representatives allows floor privileges to a very select crowd, but it was an honor granted to presidential widow Dolley Madison. Dolley liked to listen to the debate from the galleries, but it's not known whether she ever took up the offer to sit in with the boys on the floor.

Elections in the late 1700s and early 1800s were notable in New Jersey in that women were allowed to vote. The right was taken away in 1807 amidst allegations of rampant voter fraud. It was claimed that men were voting, then dressing up as women and going to vote a second time.

At least one newspaper editor approved of abolitionist and women's rights proponent Lucretia Mott because she didn't allow her activism to interfere with her housework.

Women played key roles in the abolitionist movement. The American Anti-Slavery Society formed in 1833 counted among its members Lucretia Mott, Susan. B. Anthony, and Elizabeth Cady Stanton. At the time, ending slavery seemed more possible than awarding women the right to vote. When Stanton wanted to incorporate a women's voting plank into abolitionist verbiage, Mott herself demurred, saying "Oh Lizzie, thee will make us (look) ridiculous."

> ## The World Anti-Slavery Convention, held in Britain in 1840, did not permit women.

In the first half of the 19th century, single women could generally own property, bring lawsuits, and enter into contracts. Married women generally could not.

When the 14th Amendment granted all citizens universal privileges and immunities, Susan B. Anthony took it to mean that women, being citizens, now were permitted voting privileges. In 1872, she marched into a polling place and demanded to vote. To her surprise, her request was granted. Two weeks later, however, she was arrested for illegal voting.

★

The first woman sworn into the US Senate was the (somewhat) progressive Rebecca Latimer Felton, who served for a day. After the death of Senator Thomas Watson, Felton was appointed by Georgia Governor Thomas Hardwick. Hardwick had opposed the 19th Amendment that granted women the right to vote, but after its passage faced a massive new female electorate who was not happy with him.

American women were first allowed to vote in the Wyoming territory in 1869. When Wyoming petitioned to become a state, Congress initially refused on the basis of female voting rights. Wyoming declared that it would rather remain a territory than come into the Union without women's suffrage. Congress backed down.

> The western territories had become closer and closer to allowing women the right to vote through the mid-1800s. In 1869 women's suffrage failed in the Dakota territory by a single vote.

By the end of the 19th century, four states, Wyoming, Utah, Colorado, and Idaho allowed women to vote. Since Wyoming was still a territory, Colorado wins the technical distinction of being the first state to grant women the vote.

According to one version of the story, the bill to enfranchise women began as a joke that got out of hand. Another version is that it was a play on the part of racist lawmakers to embarrass Wyoming's Republican governor, who supported voting rights for former slaves. It was hoped by these Democratic lawmakers that the governor would veto the women's suffrage bill, making him appear to be putting black men ahead of white women. (In those days Democrats were conservative and Republicans were the progressives.) A number of amendments were proposed with the intent of killing the bill.

Along with political gamesmanship, there were practical reasons for allowing women to vote. Women were in high demand on the western frontier in the second half of the 19th century, where men outnumbered women 6 to 1. Allowing women the right to vote was seen as something of a recruiting tool to lure more women to the frontier.

In Wyoming, the story didn't end with passage of women's suffrage. In fact, it was just getting interesting. Democrats assumed women would support them for giving them the vote, but in 1870 when women went to the polls for the first time in Wyoming, records indicate that about 1,000 women (much to the horror of Democrats) voted overwhelmingly for the more progressive Republicans. Women helped elect a Republican territorial representative to Congress, so the Democratic legislature decided that allowing women the vote hadn't been all that bright an idea in the first place, and voted to repeal the law. This was vetoed by the Republican governor, who also had a change of heart and was now delighted with this new, female electorate. His veto was overridden in the House, but fell one vote shy in the Senate. William Bright, the lawmaker who had originally introduced the women's suffrage bill, and a Democratic saloonkeeper, was asked some years after about all the political intrigue. He said the bill was not introduced "in fun" and didn't mention race or politics as being a factor. Instead, he said, he was motivated by the fact that his wife "was as good as any man and better than convicts and idiots."

★

Newspapers were published in the West catering to newly minted female voters. They kept abreast of political issues of the day and many of their topics would resonate today: labor law, equal pay with men, divorce law, and reproductive rights.

★

From the time women were first able to vote, it took nearly 50 years for a woman to be elected to Congress. Jeanette Rankin of Montana was elected in 1916, and upon her entrance to the capitol, newspapers were less interested in her political views than what she was wearing.

> Rankin was elected prior to women receiving the vote nationwide. On her election, she received several marriage proposals and an offer of $5,000 from a toothpaste company for a photo of her teeth.

Rankin quickly became controversial, becoming 1 of 50 representatives to oppose America's entry into WWI. "I felt the first time the first woman had a chance to say no to war, she should say it," Rankin said. She received more criticism than any of her male colleagues who voted the same way. Twenty-four years later Rankin became the only member of Congress to vote against entry into WWII. Following the vote, she had to hide out in a phone booth until police could escort her through throngs of reporters and critics to her office. Once safely there, she received an overwhelming number of angry telegrams and calls, including one from her brother who said "Montana is one hundred percent against you."

Rankin did win some grudging admiration, including from the editor of the *Kansas Emporia Gazette*, who wrote "Probably a hundred men in Congress would have liked to do what she did. Not one of them had the courage to do it. The *Gazette* entirely disagrees with the wisdom of her position. But Lord, it was a brave thing!"

Montana hasn't elected a woman to Congress since.

By 1919, when Congress passed and sent to the states the 19th Amendment guaranteeing women's suffrage, only 7 states were still denying women the vote in all elections.

Tennessee put the 19th Amendment over the top on a tight, 47–45 vote. Central to the outcome was 24-year-old state representative Harry Burn, who was set to vote against ratification until he received a letter from his mother urging him to "be a good boy" and vote in favor.

The *Remonstrance* was the name of a newsletter published by the Massachusetts Association Opposed to the Further Extension of Suffrage to Women. It was published from 1890 to 1919, and provided a forum for women who opposed female suffrage.

In 1912, Dr. Max G. Schlapp, head of the department of neuro-pathology in the Post-Graduate Medical School and Hospital of New York City and in the Cornell Medical School, wrote that nothing good would come of imposing the vote on women, and that promotion of suffrage inevitably turned good women into mouth-foaming beasts. In their defense though, it wasn't their fault, having been driven to the brink by overstimulation and the stresses of modern life: "Gentle women, naturally retiring and unassertive, become suffragists and suffragettes, and they stand boldly on a soap-box in a public square, before a motley throng, to proclaim their demands. These same women . . . approve such conduct on the part of their sisters as that of breaking up meetings, storming and insulting public men in the streets, and smashing windows. These conditions are only an evidence of a nervous distress that has become universal . . . . It is not a question of equality at all. It is one of physical difference in the sexes which forbids women from performing either factory labor or disquieting tasks."

Following passage of the 19th Amendment, male voters in Maryland sued, trying to keep the vote away from women. Their arguments were dismissed by the Supreme Court.

Today women worldwide are most highly represented in elected office in Rwanda, where they hold nearly two-thirds of the seats in the lower house.

> There are 38 nations in the world with less than 10 percent representation in their lower houses, and 4 with no women at all.

When New Zealand first allowed women to vote in 1893, nearly 80 percent of the eligible women turned out. According to a report in 1911, divorce decreased 77 percent and crime decreased 55 percent after women were permitted to vote.

In the British Isles in the 1980s, women showed why it was important to give them a voice. When their request for a dialogue over the issue of nuclear weapons was refused, they, according to an account by Sarah Hipperson, "took authorities by surprise and set the tone for a most audacious and lengthy protest that lasted 19 years."

After the British Royal Air Force installed 96 cruise missiles at its Greenham Commons base in Berkshire in 1981, 36 members of Welsh group, Women for Life on Earth, chained themselves to the base perimeter fence in protest. When this proved ineffective, they established a full-time camp that by 1982 had attracted 30,000 women to an event that ringed the base with women holding hands.

A year later, 70,000 women formed a 14-mile chain from the base to a munitions factory. In between events, women lived in the outdoor camp in primitive conditions, with no power or running water, braving all kinds of weather. They were occasionally attacked by vigilante groups and frequently evicted, but after being dispersed would move right back in. In 1991 their mission became a success when nuclear weapons were removed from the base. The camp remained active for another 9 years as a continued demonstration for peace, and organizers decided the camp should be women-only, to reinforce their importance as mothers and to represent children and future generations.

★

On New Year's Eve 1982, protesters breached base security, and 44 women danced on top of the missile silo for several hours until they were arrested and imprisoned.

★

In 1983, 200 women broke into the base dressed as teddy bears, symbolizing the childhood toy. The camp incited fear in the male-dominated establishments of government, military, and media, which referred to the camp as a "witches' coven" and suggested that if they really cared for their kids, they would be staying at home caring for them.

> The camp is now designated as a historic site.

The Dirty War was a period of state-sponsored terrorism in Argentina between 1974 and 1983, in which a right-wing military junta hunted down, tortured, and killed political dissidents on the left. Many political opponents simply disappeared and were never heard from again. Among the missing was the son of Azucena Villaflor, the wife of a labor union delegate. Following her son's disappearance, she began a tireless search, joined by other moms of missing children.

On April 30, 1977, Villaflor and a dozen other mothers marched on the Plaza de Mayo at a time when no one dared show any dissatisfaction in the government whatsoever. The Mothers of Plaza de Mayo, as they came to be known, came to march every Thursday afternoon, and organized an international information campaign to counteract junta propaganda that put a happy face on increasingly dire conditions in South America.

Eight months after their first march, on International Human Rights Day, the Mothers published a newspaper advertisement with a list of missing children. That evening, Villaflor, along with other founders of the movement, was kidnapped, tortured, and dropped from an airplane into the sea. Her remains, which were buried in an unmarked grave after washing up on shore, were identified in 2005.

The Mothers have remained a strictly women-only organization, because they believed that women were better able than men to get things done.

It's estimated that as many as 30,000 people "disappeared" during the Argentine dictatorship, and 500 infants born to women in prison were stolen. Due to the continued work of the Mothers, 137 of these children, now adults, have been identified and reintroduced to their biological families.

The same forensic group that identified Villaflor also identified the long-missing remains of Che Guevara in Bolivia in 1997.

The mothers incited fear in the male-dominated junta, which referred to them as *los locas*, or "the madwomen."

Most members of the junta are in prison today serving time for genocide and crimes against humanity.

The Mothers of Plaza de Mayo still march every Thursday at 3:30 in the afternoon in the name of human rights.

In 1938, a gang of society women chained themselves to cherry trees in Washington, D.C.'s tidal basin, where a commission had determined the Jefferson Memorial should be erected. FDR assured the women, dressed in their furs, that the beautiful cherry trees would be relocated, not chopped down. But the women would have none of it, chanting in the streets and snatching shovels out of the hands of bewildered construction workers. Roosevelt finally had the trees removed in the dead of night, and in the end the cherry-tree population in the nation's capital continued on a general trend upward.

In 2018, 84-year-old Elsie Eiler was the mayor, clerk, and treasurer in the town of Monowi, Nebraska—Population 1.

Canada's national anthem was made gender neutral in 2018 when the words "all thy sons" were changed to "all of us."

Elizabeth Gilbert was an Irish dancer born in 1821, whose performance as "Lola Montez the Spanish Dancer" captivated Bavarian King Ludwig I to the point that he gave her a castle, and commensurate administrative duties. Her liberal reforms angered the Jesuits and played a role in Ludwig's downfall in the revolutions of 1848.

> The US ranks 104th in the world in percentage of female representation in government.

In 2014, at the age of 18, Saira Blair of Martinsburg, West Virginia became the youngest person elected to a state or federal office.

One of the earliest feminists was Theodora, Empress of the Eastern Roman Empire from 527 to 548. She broke convention by speaking up at councils of war, a platform typically reserved for men. She worked for women's legal rights, shut down brothels, and outlawed sex-slave trafficking. According to a 6th century historian, no one had any doubt who was boss: "Not even the government officials could approach the Empress without expending much time and effort. They were treated like servants and kept waiting in a small, stuffy room for an endless time. After many days, some of them might at last be summoned, but going into her presence in great fear, they very quickly departed. They simply showed their respect by lying face down and touching the instep of each of her feet with their lips; there was no opportunity to speak or to make any request unless she told them to do so."

★

Catherine the Great of Russia was in fact a German who assumed the throne in 1762 after Peter III was deposed and murdered. Peter was disliked, oddly, because he ended war and enlisted reforms to help the people—angering, respectively, the military and the nobles. Catherine didn't like him either, in part no doubt because he preferred playing with his toy soldiers in bed, as opposed to using it for other purposes. It is not known if she was complicit in Peter's murder, although there is little doubt she approved of it.

★

A disciple of the Enlightenment (until the French Revolution soured her on the movement), Catherine the Great wrote comedies and fiction and was friends with European luminaries including Voltaire, whom she knew only through their written correspondence. When he died she mourned him deeply. She purchased his library from his heirs and brought it to Russia. She also was said to have imprisoned her hairdresser for 3 years to keep word from getting out about her royal dandruff, or so was the story. Another tale, perpetuated by her enemies, was that she died struggling through a bout of constipation. She in fact died of a stroke in bed.

> Catherine traveled with a portable garden that was planted wherever she stopped for the night.

Catherine was enlightened for her time and place, but still had a foot planted in the past. She was known for a battery of lovers that doubled as advisors (or vice versa) including Stanisław Poniatowski, whom she placed on the Polish throne. But his religious tolerance was too much for her, and she invaded with an army that massacred 20,000 Catholics and Jews.

CHAPTER 11
THE POLITICS OF TAXATION

Nothing drives politics and politicians quite like taxes. The modern-day aversion to taxation is by no means new, and, if anything, Congress was even cheaper in Revolutionary days than it is in the modern era, when the "tax and spend" label has sunk many an otherwise-qualified candidate.

Even when the subject of discussion is not specifically about taxation, taxation manages to raise its ugly head. Al Capone was famously convicted of tax evasion because the meat of his crimes was hard to prove (he was in Florida during the Valentine's Day massacre, and even had a note from his doctor essentially saying that at the time he was too sick to shoot anyone). Capone left no paper trails, having no bank accounts in his name and having endorsed only one check in his entire life. But his conviction on tax evasion had an unexpected consequence. The US Treasury received $1 million the following year from criminals and regular citizens alike who were scrambling to file unpaid taxes.

In ancient Egypt there was a tax on cooking oil, and the only place to buy cooking oil was from the Pharaoh. One could reuse cooking oil instead, except that was prohibited by law.

It screams of adding insult to injury, but in Rome slaves who purchased their own freedom were considered to be obtaining something of value, so the good news was that they obtained their freedom; the bad news is that they were taxed for it. In Rome urine had value as well, because the ammonia was used as a cleaning agent, so it was collected and, yes, taxed.

> Taxpayers in the Inca nation paid their bills through physical labor.

Rep. Ed Orcutt of Washington State proposed a bicycle tax because the exertion of cyclists causes them to "exercise and breathe hard and therefore exhale more CO_2," ergo, bicycling is bad for the environment.

Beards were taxed by England's Henry VIII, even though he wore a beard himself. His daughter Elizabeth continued the beard tax, although guys who enjoyed the scruffy look got off free, because up to a two-week growth was not considered to be a full beard. There is little modern record of these taxes, and they were believed to be poorly enforced. Not so in Russia under Peter the Great, where the authorities would hold a man down and roughly chop off his whiskers if he couldn't produce a token indicating he had paid a beard tax. Peter's reasoning was that beards made Russia's populace seem backward compared to modern, clean-shaven Europeans. For Russians it could be a tough call on religious grounds, since the state wanted them to be clean-shaven, while their God wanted them to grow beards.

Few taxes have been more popular (among governments) and unpopular (among people) than levies on salt. After dabbling in salt taxes, France passed a permanent tax on salt in 1341, and it more or less remained in continuous effect for centuries. The government maintained a monopoly on salt, and further, required everyone over the age of 8 to buy a weekly minimum. This salt was for personal use, and could not be used in the production of salted foods. Anyone who did was charged with "salt fraud," the penalty for which on the second offense could be death.

★

Salt taxes were particularly unpopular in France, since salt is so essential in the making of cheese. The French tax on salt was finally repealed when France was liberated from the Nazis in 1945.

Smuggling of salt was common in pre-Revolutionary France, particularly by women who packed salt under their dresses in "false derrieres." The salt police, who were uniformly despised, would grope pretty girls under the guise of checking for illicit salt.

The salt tax was a factor in the 1789 French Revolution not only for the financial burden, but because 3,000 people a year were imprisoned, sent to the galleys, or executed for salt-related crimes. Revolutionaries ended the tax and freed those who were doing time on a salt rap, but the tax was restored in 1804 by Napoleon.

In China, salt was money—literally. Marco Polo reported that in salt-rich regions where currency was short, the mineral was compacted into bricks and used in place of cash. In the 1300s, salt made a fortune for Government Salt Superintendents who collected salt taxes, underreported the income, and kept a nice chunk for themselves. If it counts for anything, these superintendents sometimes put their wealth to good cultural use. In 1705, Cao Yin compiled and published *The Complete Poems of the Tang Dynasty*, a project underwritten by the Salt Administration.

> Salt taxes helped build the Great Wall of China.

The 1911 Chinese Revolution toppled the imperial rule that had endured for centuries; but the salt syndicate survived.

To shore up central finances following the revolution, the Chinese appealed to foreign bankers, who agreed to loans that were backed to a significant degree by salt, under the auspices of a new agency, the Sino-Foreign Salt Administration.

India has a long history of salt taxes, and in 1891 Mahatma Gandhi blamed an increase in leprosy on the salt tax, due to people being able to afford less of the mineral. In the spring of 1930, he and 78 of his followers trekked 240 miles in what became known as the Salt March, to protest British control and taxation of salt.

Many joined with Gandhi on the march, and many more engaged in protests over salt and, ultimately, British rule. More than 60,000 were arrested in salt protests, which failed to win any meaningful concessions, but opened the world's eyes to the cause of Indian independence.

In 1648, a tax on salt in Russia led to a riot that killed as many as 2,000 people, burned 24,000 homes, and left half of Moscow in ruins. The tax was the last straw for a public that was already fed up with corruption and inequity. Taxation largely fell on lower classes because the aristocrats had figured out loopholes that lowered their obligation, shifting the burden to poorer townspeople. The salt tax was passed to make up for tax dodges of the wealthy, but hit particularly hard since salt was essential for curing fish—a staple in the Russian diet. At first it appeared the riot would lead to progressive change, but soon the old order was restored, even stronger than before. Laws were passed that solidified the feudal system of centuries. The new code of laws had to be distributed far and wide, so in order to spread the word, Russia imported the one progressive item to come out of the Salt Riots—the printing press.

In New York, an uncut bagel is tax free. But if it is cut in half it is subjected to an 8 percent tax.

Illinois has a 1 percent tax on food, and a 5 percent tax on candy. Candy that has flour, however, is considered a food product, so it skirts the 5 percent candy tax.

New Mexico suspends state tax on residents after they have celebrated their 100th birthday.

In 1885, Canada passed a "Chinese Head Tax," on Chinese immigrants. In 1923 the tax became unnecessary when Canada banned Chinese people altogether.

In the annals of "a waste of taxpayers' dollars," few things drew as much head as Secretary of State William Seward's plan to buy Alaska at 2 cents an acre for a total of $7.2 million. It was known as Seward's Folly, but also as Seward's Icebox and Seward's Polar Bear Garden. Critics said we were about to spend $7.2 million on glaciers and walruses. Newspaper editor Horace Greely said the money should be used to reduce taxes, not to buy land. One senator said he would only vote for the purchase of Alaska if Seward would agree to go live there. The treaty went to the Committee of Foreign Relations, chaired by Sen. Charles Sumner. Sumner was little more inclined to vote in favor of the transaction than anyone else, but he was blessed with that rarest of commodities, an open mind. He spent an extraordinary amount of time researching the territory, and this herculean effort that few others would have engaged in, completely changed his mind. On the Senate floor, he outlined the value of Alaska's resources with such clarity that the measure passed 37–2.

Just over a decade prior to passage of the Alaska Purchase Treaty, Sumner had been beaten nearly to death on the Senate floor by a South Carolina congressman. Had Sumner not eventually recovered—and for a long time it was touch and go—Alaska might not be a state today.

A number of European nations have a tax on religion, which helps pay church expenses. They are usually less than 2 percent and sometimes subtracted from federal income taxes and sent to the denomination of the taxpayer. Before Christianity swept Europe, Germanic tribal leaders (effectively the state) financially supported religious rites (the church). As Christianity took over, this practice continued out of custom, even at times that the secular rulers and the Pope weren't particularly getting along.

In Austria, the church tax was implemented in 1939 by Adolf Hitler. It was continued after the war in order to keep the church independent of politics. Before it was changed in 2003, resignation from the church (and its taxes) in Austria required a written form and a waiting period for the soon-to-be former parishioner to think over his decision.

In Germany, 70 percent of church income comes from the church tax. Those who belong to a nonreligious spiritual organization are charged a "cult tax." Church members are free to leave the church and affiliated taxation behind, but sometimes they then have trouble finding someone to marry and bury them.

In 2004, Italy used a share of its church taxes to help invade Iraq.

> America might try this with its ubiquitous political pollsters: in 2010, the Romanian Senate introduced legislation to tax witches, soothsayers, and fortune tellers, penalizing them if their visions did not come true.

Taxes have led to revolts and revolutions, but in one case taxes changed the entire course of western political society. The tax that started it all was created in England by Henry I and was known as scutage. This tax was a way for knights to buy their way out of military service. As mercenaries came into greater use, this was a win-win, since to the king, the money was more valuable than the manpower. The status quo might have been maintained had King John not raised the scutage by 300 percent—and in peacetime, no less—leading to the rebellion of 1215 and the issuing of the Magna Carta.

A cat-and-mouse game has always existed between tax-payer and tax collector. England placed a tax on fireplaces in the 1600s under the logical theory that the larger the home, the more fireplaces it would have, so residents began to brick up their fireplaces to hide them from the tax collector. In the 1700s, England placed a tax on bricks. Since the tax was on a per-brick basis, builders began making bigger bricks, so the government made the brick tax progressive, sort of, in that the bigger the brick, the bigger the tax. But by 1850 the government gave up and repealed the brick tax. Also repealed in the 1850s was a tax on windows. Homeowners had predictably dodged this one by building windowless homes, which the government soon realized caused a rather significant health problem. A tax on printed wallpaper was avoided by builders who hung paper and then painted the paper.

England taxes televisions and uses the proceeds to fund the BBC. A totally blind TV owner still must pay half the tax.

> In Oregon, double amputees get a $50 tax credit.

Lawmakers have a saying, "Don't tax you, don't tax me, tax that man behind the tree." For practical political purposes, the man behind the tree is often engaged in a behavior upon which the majority of the populace frowns. These "sin taxes" are applied to drinking, gambling, smoking, and the like. The federal government gets 3 percent of its budget, or about $100 billion from excise taxes that are primarily receipts on gambling, and alcohol. States collect about 4 percent of their budgets from sin taxes, or about $33 billion.

Sin taxes are politically popular, even if the item being taxed is popular too. In 2017, 57 percent of Americans favored a soda tax, so long as the proceeds benefitted children's health.

Politicians frequently justify sin taxes by saying revenue will be used for treatment and prevention. But just 3 percent of state tobacco revenues go to prevention.

Some complain that governments don't really want to end the sin, since the tax on the sin is such a boon to the treasury. In China, at least, they would be right. In 2009, residents of China's Hubei province faced fines if they did not smoke cigarettes. That's because the government was short on money and needed the tobacco tax. Quotas dictated the number of cigarettes that needed to be smoked, and apparently the scheme worked because today Chinese citizens smoke 1 out of every 3 cigarettes produced in the world. China is now trying to end the habit it fueled by making smoking in public illegal.

England stopped taxing playing cards in 1960.

The states with the lowest taxes on cigarettes tend to be the ones with the highest percentage of smokers, led by Kentucky, where 26 percent of the citizens smoke.

In 1980, the average price of a pack of cigarettes was 60 cents. In 2018, Hawaii charged $3.20 a pack just in tax.

In 1983, the federal government raised taxes on cigarettes by 10 percent. Tobacco companies responded in preparation by raising the prices of cigarettes gradually over the course of 1982 (and then eating the new federal tax) to keep smokers from getting sticker shock and quitting.

A 10 percent tax on cigarettes decreases demand by 4 percent.

The city of Johnstown, Pennsylvania had a history of devastating floods, so in 1936 the state passed a liquor tax to pay for repairs to the town. Enough money to do the work was collected by 1942, but the state did not repeal the tax, which today brings in $200 million a year.

Pennsylvania also taxes coin-operated vacuum cleaners. The Keystone state also taxes pumpkins, but, as do Iowa and New Jersey, only those that are to be carved instead of eaten.

For every dollar states spend on treatment and prevention of substance abuse, they spend $60 on punishment.

Marijuana taxes and fees in Colorado totaled $66 million in 2014. By 2017 they totaled $247 million.

A number of states tax marijuana sales, even though they are illegal.

The IRS has instructions in its procedural manual for collecting taxes in event of nuclear war.

In 2007, Florida became the first state to offer a back-to-school sales tax holiday. By 2018, 17 states had tax holidays, down from a peak of 19. Studies show the holidays do not always benefit the consumer because when the states lower taxes, retailers raise prices.

Mississippi's August tax holiday includes a break on ammunition and firearms.

In a case of biting the hand that feeds, Maine taxes blueberries, and Kentucky taxes Thoroughbred stud fees.

> The IRS instructs taxpayers to report the value of stolen property as income.

Poll taxes are often associated with discrimination, but early in the nation's history they were thought of as a tax on citizenship. In the colony of Massachusetts, between a third and a half of its budget was funded by poll taxes. Poll taxes became popular in the South during the Jim Crow era and after the 15th Amendment guaranteed all races the right to vote.

Texas levies a tax on strip clubs, which has come to be known as a pole tax.

Caribbean governments have a well-deserved reputation as tax dodges for the wealthy, but, after decades as champion, the king of the hill is still Switzerland. The Swiss passed a law in 1934 criminalizing the divulgence of bank records, and today the Swiss hold more than a quarter of the world's offshore wealth. Some suspect that the inspiration behind the secrecy is that Switzerland may get a slice of the cash—but of course the Swiss are understandably tight-lipped about this as well.

Aside from secrecy, Switzerland's currency is solid; there is no inflation, interest accrues tax free, gold holdings represent 40 percent of banking receipts, accounts are guaranteed—and Switzerland hasn't been in a war since 1505.

Switzerland's secrecy in not always ironclad. The Swiss cooperate on criminal cases, and in 2009 a landmark case prompted the largest Swiss bank to reveal the names of a few hundred clients who had been dodging US taxes.

Artists and writers in Ireland pay no tax on their income unless they are wealthy.

> **In Denmark, cows are taxed up to $110 to compensate for the greenhouse gases they emit.**

For children who spend Saturday mornings watching cartoons and shoveling down spoonsful of sugary flakes, possibly the best tax break ever is the one in Canada which exempts cereal manufacturers that include a toy in the box. But only, and this is important, if the toy isn't a derivative of "beer, liquor, or wine."

In Germany, bribery was (somewhat) legal until 2002. Even better for those of certain political proclivities, is that bribes were tax deductible. There were some strings. The people participating in the bribery needed to be named, and they could not yet have been caught. Germany ended the tax deduction 3 years before it ended the bribes.

Residents of Monaco, a nation about the size of New York's Central Park, are forbidden from entering their storied casinos. The upside is that they do not pay any income tax.

CHAPTER 12
THE POLITICS OF DRINK

The problem with alcohol, said Abraham Lincoln, did not concern the use of a bad thing, but the abuse of a good thing. Certainly, that sentiment applied to politics, where liquor (or the absence thereof) has been blamed for governmental dysfunction. Lincoln himself owned a liquor license, although he had plenty of opportunity to see the downside of the industry as well.

Some believe the whiskey that fueled the savagery of politicians, preachers, and newspaper editors was responsible for the Civil War. Stories abound of the "fire eaters" on the wharfs of Charleston, South Carolina chugging down whiskey and whipping the crowds into a frenzy. A judge once remarked that South Carolina's problem was that it was too small to be its own nation, and too large to be a lunatic asylum.

Yet as gridlock and a lack of cooperation have infected modern politics, some believe the new, drier Congress might be to blame. Former Mississippi Governor Haley Barbour recalled his visits to Congress when he was in college, seeing lawmakers from North and South, East and West, liberal and conservative, sitting around together socializing and sipping cocktails.

★

Winston Churchill swilled champagne in the war department and tartly dismissed any concerns of excess, saying "I took more out of drink than drink took out of me."

> ## Adolf Hitler, Churchill's nemesis, didn't drink.

In Ireland, President Bill Clinton was handed a pint of Guinness for a photo op, and was immediately interrupted by a Guinness representative who broke the moment by giving him a kiss. The *Guardian* newspaper said this was a win-win for Clinton, who liked women more than beer and had tastes that, at the time, ran toward "junk food, cigars, and the odd Scotch."

Prior to the Dayton conference on Bosnia in the early 1990s, US envoy Richard Holbrooke was amazed at the alcohol consumption of Slobodan Milosevic, who seemed to survive on Scotch, wine, and plum brandy. "I saw no evidence then, or later, that the alcohol affected Milosevic's judgment," he said. "The Americans drank little, and I began a policy of accepting Milosevic's frequent offers of drinks only when we had reached agreements."

Arab hosts frequently offer alcohol at diplomatic events even though, for them, drinking is forbidden.

In 1994, Russian Federation President Boris Yeltsin landed at Shannon Airport for a meeting with Irish Prime Minister Albert Reynolds. At the foot of the plane were 31 official vehicles, an Air Force band, and an honor guard of 100 soldiers of the 12th Infantry Battalion. But the Irish never saw Yeltsin, who was presumed to be too drunk to disembark.

While politicians frequently deride the effects of drink, they do not turn away the tax money it generates. "The government," said Derek Rutherford of the British Institute of Alcohol Studies," is more dependent on alcohol than any alcoholic."

No doubt when the Constitution was ratified there was relief on all sides, but even so the beverage list was considerable: 8 bottles of whiskey, 60 bottles of claret, 54 bottles of Madeira, 22 bottles of port, 12 jugs of beer, and 8 bottles of hard cider. To make sure no one went short, there were 7 bowls of alcoholic punch. The bowls were so big that, according to a popular account, "ducks could swim in them."

John Adams began each day with a large mug of hard cider. Although he never showed signs of being drunk, he feared that a lack of access to alcohol would make him sick.

> In early America, candidates were expected to get drunk alongside the people to show that they were "one of the guys" and not some aristocratic tool.

Elections in America were often decided by which candidate provided the most liquor. After losing his first election, George Washington made sure it didn't happen again, by supplying voters with 144 gallons of booze.

A popular Russian joke in the 1990s went like this:

A man stood in a half-mile long line outside a liquor store
on the outskirts of Moscow waiting to buy some vodka.

"That's it," he says impatiently to his friend. "I'm off to the
Kremlin to kill Gorbachev."

He sets off to murder the Soviet leader. An hour later, he
returns.

"Did you kill him?" his friend asks.

"Kill him?" the man replies, "That line was longer than this
one."

Dinh La Thang, the former Communist Party leader of Ho Chi
Minh City who was dismissed from the Vietnamese Politburo in
2017, was arrested over "economic mismanagement," specifically a
thirst for Macallan 30, a Scotch whisky that costs around $2,000
a bottle.

★

Grover Cleveland averaged 6 to 8 beers a day, but during a con-
test for district attorney earlier in his career, he and his opponent,
Lyman K. Bass, agreed to limit their consumption to 4 glasses of
beer a day. When this proved difficult, they agreed to "borrow"
against days leading up to the election. When those ran out, they
reset the clock and brought glasses the size of pitchers to the saloon,
and this made things satisfactory.

In the early days of the nation, heavy drinking was the norm. This was not entirely insane, because distilled and brewed spirits could be safer than water, which was frequently polluted in cities that had little in the way of sanitation, so people were seldom rebuked for knocking back the sauce at all hours of the day. But there were limits, such as when Revolutionary officer Adam Stephen got so drunk on his march to battle outside of Philadelphia that he wound up getting confused and attacking his own side.

The temperance movement, which came along toward the end of the 19th century, tried to deny that our founding heroes were on such good terms with alcohol. One famous painting of George Washington was doctored during the temperance movement by painting out a bottle of liquor on the table.

★

The most important product on the American frontier in the late 1700s was whiskey. While it was not cost-effective to haul a wagonload of grain to market across the rugged Allegheny Mountains, corn or rye that was distilled into alcohol was the ultimate value-added crop. It was not only a relaxant, but also a medicine, painkiller, and, perhaps unwittingly, a disinfectant. It returned hard currency to a region that had none, and even served as currency itself, so naturally, the first thing the young American government wanted to tax, in 1791, was whiskey. The result was predictable. The men of Western Pennsylvania rebelled, with an army consisting of as many as 7,000 soldiers marching under a flag of independence. The movement was put down without excessive bloodshed by President George Washington himself, who led 13,000 militia members into Western Pennsylvania.

The largest whiskey distiller in America at the time was—George Washington. Because of the way the tax was structured, large producers paid a third less tax than small producers.

Western farmers were further penalized because Spain (which owned the Louisiana Territory at the time) prohibited them from commercial shipping on the Mississippi River.

Many of the pioneer distillers were Revolutionary War veterans, who felt subjected to the very thing they'd been fighting against: taxation without representation. Other rebels just liked being rebels and went after wealthy residents of Pittsburgh whether they had any connection to the government, or whiskey, or anything that was really worth fighting about. Some felt Pittsburgh was another "Sodom" and ought to be burned to the ground just on general principles.

The rebel force melted into the backcountry at Washington's show of force. But he couldn't lead an army over the mountains every day, and for many distillers the happy solution was simply to refuse to pay the tax, an act of disobedience the government could do little about.

If Washington's men didn't find anyone to fight, they didn't find anything to eat, either. Storehouses had all been stripped in advance, forcing the militia to steal from local farmers, giving the force the nickname of the Watermelon Army.

The Whiskey Tax came to define the Democratic and Federalist parties: the Federalists being the tax-and-spend type, and the Democrats being advocates of small, inexpensive government, uninterested in building things like roads. Thomas Jefferson was representative of the latter, and in 1800, largely aided by those who rebelled against the whiskey tax, Jefferson won the presidency. Congress repealed the Whiskey Tax 2 years later.

North Korea says they have developed a rice wine that causes no hangover.

In the 1950s, the French tried to "modernize" Vietnam by getting them to switch from rice liquor to beer.

> While debating Prohibition legislation, congressmen would, with some frequency, adjourn for cocktails.

Bootlegging was rampant during Prohibition, and Congress was not immune. Through the decade of the 1920s, George Cassiday, a failed West Virginia railroad worker, served Congress after being told that politicians paid a better price for hooch than most anyone else. "The man in the green hat," as he came to be known, worked out of an office he had been given in the Capitol Building. His first two customers were Southern congressmen who had voted for Prohibition. Cassiday later said his customers included 4 of every 5 members of the House and Senate.

Following his arrest in 1930 Cassiday gave up bootlegging and wrote in the *Washington Post*, "Considering that I took the risk and did the leg work from 1920 to 1930, I am more than willing to let the general public decide how I stack up with the senator or representative who ordered the stuff and consumed it on the premises." The general public did just that. In the mid-term elections voters threw out "dry" Republicans and replaced them with "wet" Democrats.

President Warren Harding's attorney general arranged for the Justice Department to sneak cases of seized alcohol into his own personal liquor closet.

People tolerated Representative Andrew Volstead, the "father of prohibition," so long as all that happened was talk. But when he actually was able to make Prohibition the law of the land under the Volstead Act, he was voted out of office.

Not all states went along with the federal government's new path. Kansas remained dry, to the point that the state attorney general maintained that passengers on a commercial airline should not be allowed to drink while in Kansas airspace.

Franklin D. Roosevelt won election in no small part because he promised to end Prohibition. At the end of Prohibition, Roosevelt proclaimed "What America needs now is a drink."

Roosevelt himself seldom had more than a couple of cocktails—unless he found himself in the presence of Winston Churchill, which is why Eleanor felt the British prime minister was a bad influence.

★

Told that General Ulysses Grant was a heavy drinker, President Lincoln purportedly asked his aides to find out what brand Grant partook of and send it to his other generals, few of whom to that point had enjoyed much success. Grant's drinking has probably been exaggerated, as accounts generally give him credit for being sober during his campaigns.

> **After the war, many surviving Civil War generals had a brand of whiskey named after them.**

The Bowery in New York City was famous for its saloons, but the political bosses at the very top generally left the rowdy drinking to their lieutenants and constituents. Even after a big election victory, they sipped seltzer water at the victory parties and were back hard at work early the next morning.

According to a study examining states through the second half of the 20th century, states that became more liberal politically saw, perhaps counterintuitively, an increase in their consumption of beer and liquor, while wine consumption tended to fall.

President Lyndon Johnson's favorite drink was Scotch, and occasionally his bartenders—in the form of Secret Servicemen—would come along when he decided to go for a drive. According to his special assistant, Joseph A. Califano, Jr., "In the early afternoon, the President, with me next to him in the front seat, took his white Lincoln convertible, top down, for a drive around the ranch. It was incredibly hot; the dust clouds made it hard to breathe. But there was relief. As we drove around, we were followed by a car and a station wagon with Secret Service agents. The President drank Cutty Sark scotch and soda out of a large white plastic foam cup. Periodically, Johnson would slow down and hold his left arm outside the car, shaking the cup and ice. A Secret Service agent would run up to the car, take the cup, and go back to the station wagon. There another agent would refill it with ice, scotch, and soda as the first agent trotted behind the wagon. Then the first agent would run the refilled cup up to LBJ's outstretched and waiting hand, as the President's car moved slowly along."

★

President Richard Nixon had a notoriously low tolerance for alcohol, a fact that did not preclude him from imbibing. During the Yom Kippur War, his aides covered for him when he was indisposed, according to a 1973 phone transcript between his assistant Brent Snowcroft and Secretary of State Henry Kissinger:

Snowcroft: "The switchboard just got a call from 10 Downing Street to inquire whether the president would be available for a call from the Prime Minister within 30 minutes. The subject would be the Middle East."

Kissinger: "Can we tell them no? When I talked with the president he was loaded."

> In April 1969, North Korea shot down a US spy plane. A drunken and enraged Nixon ordered plans for a tactical nuclear strike, but Kissinger quietly spoke to military leaders, telling them not to act until the president sobered up.

In 1940, House Speaker Nicholas Longworth set up a secret drinking hideout, with a guard outside the unmarked door and plenty of bourbon within. The club, notorious for loosening the tongues of younger members, was known as the Board of Education.

President Jimmy Carter frowned on drink, but he couldn't do much about his family. His headline hogging, unabashedly redneck brother came out with his own brand of beer named after himself, Billy. Even Jimmy's mother Lilian insisted she was not "square" because she enjoyed her bourbon.

Senator Teddy Kennedy had his issues with Carter, not the least of which being that Jimmy and Rosalynn had all the liquor removed from the White House, making for many a dry evening.

Carter also tried to eliminate the tax break for an American institution, the three-martini lunch. Gerald Ford, the man he beat, dismissed Carter's idea, saying, "where else can you get an ear full, a belly full, and a snoot full?"

In 1855, Chicago Mayor Levi Boone had an imaginative way to combat immigration, of which he was not in favor. Boone had come to power on the platform of the Know Nothing political party, which despised immigrants and Catholics, and just about anyone else who wasn't a white American Protestant. The unwanted immigrants at this point in time were the Germans and Irish, who worked hard 6 days a week, and spent Sundays relaxing with a brew (or 6) in the local beer garden. Boone raised the cost of a liquor license from $50 to $300 and began to enforce an old ordinance preventing taverns from opening on Sundays. These actions, in the near term, led to the Lager Beer Riot, in which throngs of immigrants stormed the city in protest of what they believed to be discriminatory actions. But long term, the immigrants united and, unlike in the previous election, showed up at the polls and voted out the Know Nothings.

CHAPTER 13
THE POLITICS
OF RELIGION

The notion that government ought to keep its mitts off of religion and vice versa is of course relatively new. Ancient and not-so ancient governments alike would have been puzzled by the separation of church and state since they would have been hard pressed to see a difference between the two.

Christ himself suggested each should keep its own house when he advised to "render unto Caesar the things that are Caesar's and unto God the things that are God's." But religion being religion, there is sharp disagreement over the meaning of that quote.

Kings felt that they had direct control over the state and indirect control over religion; popes have believed they have direct control of religion and indirect control over the state. Both have, through the years, taken their right to govern directly from the Almighty, a power they have been more than happy to run with.

The thread that led to separation of church and state ran from St. Augustine to Martin Luther to James Madison, the doctrine becoming more accentuated with each subsequent revision. But even today, the separation exists primarily in a strict legal sense, as even our national pledges, songs, and coinage make reference to spirituality. And of course, through most of world history, religion's influence on politics has run much deeper than a slogan.

State-sponsored religions seldom work out well for minority practitioners, and nowhere was this more evident than the Spanish Inquisition. Prior to the Inquisition, Christians, Muslims, and Jews had lived side by side in Spain in relative peace. The Inquisition changed this, with as many as 150,000 people being prosecuted and between 3,000 and 5,000 put to death.

The Spanish Inquisition was ordered by the Pope at the end of the 12th century and was targeted toward a sect of Christians in the south of France that believed in two Gods: The "Good God" of the New Testament and the "Bad God" of the Old.

The Inquisition may have had as much to do with politics as religion. By the 14th century, England and France had expelled their Jewish populations, rendering Spain's tolerance of other religions suspect in the eyes of greater Europe. A European nation that hoped to be a player on the world stage needed to be Christian. Furthermore, King Ferdinand feared an attack by the Ottoman Empire might be aided and abetted by Muslims within his own country. And of course, money played a role. Jews were frequently more successful at banking and business than their Christian counterparts, which caused resentment.

> Ferdinand and Isabella named Tomás de Torquemada the first Inquisitor. Torquemada spent 15 years as Grand Inquisitor before his zeal became too much, even for the pope.

The chief targets of the Inquisitor were Jews who only pretended to convert in order to escape persecution. To catch these people, the church encouraged people to spy on their neighbors and turn in anyone who might be doing something suspicious, such as cleaning their homes on Friday.

★

Although known for their ruthlessness, Spanish inquisitors provided multiple opportunities for heretics to refute the charges. Once this lengthy appeal process was over, the victims could still convert. If they did not, they were subjected to torture, and if they still did not convert, they were burned at the stake.

> Heretics were tortured with an early form of waterboarding.

Those burned at the stake were subjected to a public spectacle known as an act of faith, or *auto-da-fe* that drew huge crowds. Heretics who recanted and kissed the cross were strangled before being burnt. Those who just recanted were burned with seasoned wood that burned faster. Those who did neither were burned with green wood, which drew out the process.

The Inquisition was not abolished until 1834. By that time, the exodus of Jewish talent had ruined Spain as a world power.

The Spanish Inquisition has been greatly, and perhaps oddly parodied in comedy, including Monty Python's bit "Nobody expects the Spanish Inquisition," to Mel Brooks playing Torquemada in *History of the World Part I* to Gilbert and Sullivan's musical routine, "What a day, what a day for an *auto-da-fe.*"

Many American Quakers boycotted cotton and sugar because they were the products of slavery.

"In God We Trust" has been one of America's defining mottos and, some would say, one of our defining principles. It began on the 1864 two-cent piece, the work of Treasury Secretary Salmon P. Chase acting on the advice of a Pennsylvania preacher, but it wasn't until the Cold War that "In God We Trust" replaced *E Pluribus Unum* as the national motto, as a direct response to the atheism of the Soviet Union. Not all American statesmen have been on board with the motto either. Teddy Roosevelt thought it a mad idea to mention the Almighty on our currency, but was voted down by Congress in 1908, when they required the words be included on America's money. Roosevelt's stated opinion was that it would cheapen God by splashing his name all over coins, stamps, or public ads.

Outside of TR, at least ten American US presidents were not particularly religious. They included Thomas Jefferson, James Monroe, and Abraham Lincoln.

Laws in seven states—Arkansas, Maryland, Mississippi, North Carolina, South Carolina, Tennessee, and Texas—prohibit atheists from holding public office. Mississippi's Constitution says, "No person who denies the existence of a Supreme Being shall hold any office in this state." North Carolina's says, "The following persons shall be disqualified for office: First, any person who shall deny the being of Almighty God." In Maryland an atheist bookkeeper had to go all the way to the Supreme Court in 1961 before he was allowed to become a notary public.

Thomas Jefferson was a tinkerer, so whatever his religious views might have been, he still couldn't resist the temptation to improve on the Holy Scriptures. He cut-and-pasted the gospels with a sharp blade and glue to produce what has become known as the "Jefferson Bible." He believed Matthew, Mark, Luke, and John trafficked in fake news, and his version leaves out all the events that do not stand up to reason, like the story in which Jesus blesses a scant amount of bread and fish and suddenly it multiplies into a quantity sufficient to feed a multitude.

★

In 2005, a French court banned an advertisement by a clothing designer that stylized the Last Supper and depicted Christ as a woman. The judge ruled the ad was "a gratuitous and aggressive act of intrusion on people's innermost beliefs." A lawyer for the Catholic Church, which asked for the injunction, feared that "Tomorrow, Christ on the cross will be selling socks."

In 988 Vladimir the Great wanted to unify all of Russia under a single belief, so he went religion shopping. The available options were Islam, Judaism, the Catholic Christianity of Western Europe, and the Orthodox Christianity of Eastern Europe. Like, perhaps, many people today, Vlad liked the idea of religion more than he liked religion itself, what with all its rules and conditions. The hard drinking, hard feasting ruler was not one to deny himself of worldly pleasures, which made some of the religions inconvenient. He had, legend has it, settled on Islam until he discovered it frowned on drink. Same with Judaism and its rules regarding pork and diet in general. It was the Cathedral of Hagia Sophia in Constantinople that seemingly turned the tide—the ceremony and splendor satisfied his apparent need for excess.

A Russian sect founded in 2007 called The Chapel of Russia's Resurrection believes Vladimir Putin is the reincarnation of both Vladimir the Great and the Apostle Paul. The all-female sect believes Putin, like Paul, started out as a persecutor of Christians but became infused with the Holy Spirit. Putin's press secretary, when asked about the sect, noncommittally stated, "It is impressive that they think so highly of [Putin's] work."

Saddam Hussein also was something of a latecomer to religion, embracing it only after his son survived an assassination attempt. Never one for half measures, however, in the 1990s Saddam commissioned a calligrapher to make a beautiful reproduction of the Quran—written in the tyrant's own blood. Saddam supposedly donated 50 pints of blood to have the work created, but there are questions whether he donated any at all and whether his devotion was genuine or whether the whole thing was a publicity stunt. The Blood Quran remains secreted away, with no one having any idea what to do with it.

After winning power in 1957, Haiti's Francois "Papa Doc" Duvalier practiced on voodoo in order to keep it. He claimed to have placed a curse on JFK that led to his assassination, and altered the words of the Lord's Prayer to make himself the hero instead of God.

Vatican City is the world's smallest nation, with the smallest population. It is an absolute monarchy with the Pope as sovereign. The European Union says that to join, a candidate must be a free market democracy. Being a theocracy, Vatican City doesn't qualify, but because it is so small, and surrounded by an EU state, it gets a pass. When a reporter once asked Pope John XXIII how many people worked in the Vatican, he replied "About half of them."

A "Hot Priest Calendar" can be found on gift stands around the Vatican depicting the city's hunkiest clergymen.

> The Vatican bank has the
> only ATM in the world with
> transaction instructions in Latin.

Gregorio Allegri's song Miserere, composed in the 1630s during the reign of Pope Urban VIII, was only to be used for certain ceremonies and it was forbidden for it to be transcribed, an act that was punishable by excommunication. At age 14, Mozart listened to it twice and jotted it down from memory, thereby providing the world with its first bootlegged copy of the masterpiece.

In 1985, five Americans were arrested in Vatican City for displaying satanic hand signals, which later turned out to be the University of Texas's demonstration for Hook 'em Horns.

Known as the "Holy Prepuce," a number of churches in Europe have claimed to possess Jesus's foreskin. Often these claims have overlapped, so to speak. In the 1600s, a Vatican librarian wrote a white paper entitled *De Praeputio Domini Nostri Jesu Christi Diatriba* (A Discussion of the Foreskin of Our Lord Jesus Christ). His theory was that Jesus's foreskin was not in any church. It had, in fact, risen like Christ and had become the rings of the planet Saturn.

The Vatican has acknowledged that Galileo was correct, and that the Earth was not the center of the solar system. It did so in 1992.

James Oglethorpe, founder of the colony of Georgia, wanted to form a region safe from the items that caused others so much trouble, so he banned liquor, lawyers, slavery—and Catholics. If the first three prohibitions make sense, the fourth seemed strange for a territory noted for toleration. The reasoning was that Oglethorpe didn't so much want to ban Catholics as he wanted to ban Spanish spies infiltrating from Florida.

Huey Long, Louisiana's populist "Kingfish," frequently gave speeches with a Bible in his hand, quoting from the book he claimed to have read more times than he could count. His brother later said the only verses the Kingfish knew were the ones his mother had read to them when they were children.

At the top of the Washington Monument, facing east, is the inscription "Laus Deo," Latin for "praise God."

In the 2014 election, according to exit polls, those who go to church at least once a week voted for Republicans over Democrats for the House of Representatives by a 58 percent to 40 percent margin. Those who never attend services voted Democratic by a margin of 62 percent to 36 percent. In only 10 states do more than half the people routinely go to church. All but one, Utah, are in the South. Vermont is the only state where fewer than 25 percent of the people regularly attend church.

> **Nationwide, 71 percent of Americans profess to be Christian, a religion that is held by 92 percent of the members of Congress.**

In 2014, only one member of Congress, Representative Kyrsten Sinema, an Arizona Democrat, claimed no religious affiliation.

CHAPTER 14
POLITICS AND CORRUPTION

Let's face it, politics would be far less interesting without corruption—boring even. Without greed, and anger over greed, politics would be a limp dishrag relegated to sopping up grey water of public duties and wringing it off the front porch into a bucket of banality. A sewer project, for example, is of no interest to anyone until money that should be spent on pipes goes into someone's pocket. Then the project becomes fascinating.

At local levels, more than a few have entered politics out of purely selfish motivations—perhaps they want to run that sewer line past their own property to increase its value, for example. But on the larger stage, politicians more often have nobler ideals in mind. It is only after being exposed to the campaign money of lobbyists and the power of the office that their moral compass fails them.

Yet even the most corrupt can be doing good here and there, and often times a lot of it. The much-maligned Tammany Hall of New York City ran what amounted to a welfare system for destitute immigrants arriving on American shores. Tammany politician George Washington Plunkitt claimed to have assisted the victims of a house fire; secured the release of 6 drunks from the pokey by speaking on their behalf to a judge; paid the rent of a poor family to prevent their eviction and gave them money for food; secured employment for 4 individuals; attended the funerals of two of his constituents (one Italian, the other Jewish); attended a Bar Mitzvah; and attended the wedding of a Jewish couple from his ward—all in the course of a single day.

Illinois Secretary of State Paul Powell was once quoted as saying, "There's only one thing worse than a defeated politician, and that's a broke one." So he made sure he wasn't. In the 1960s Illinois residents paying the fee for a driver's license would make their checks out not to the DMV, but to Secretary of State Paul Powell.

★

Who would have thought, but these checks did not necessarily end up in the state treasury. When he died of a heart attack in 1970, investigators found $800,000 in cash in his Springfield hotel room, much of it stuffed in shoeboxes. Illinois Senator Adlai Stevenson III later said that "Paul Powell left behind some pretty big shoe boxes to fill."

There's something about the Land of Lincoln and drivers' licenses. After a 1994 traffic accident left 6 children dead, an investigation revealed that the driver at fault seemed to have little grasp of English or anything involving the rules of the road. Further inquiry determined that Secretary of State George Ryan's office was selling licenses to truck drivers regardless of their qualifications. For Ryan, it was the tip of the iceberg. He was eventually convicted on 22 counts including racketeering, bribery, money laundering, extortion, and tax fraud.

The known record for bribe-taking in Congress belongs to Randy "Duke" Cunningham, who, as a member of a House appropriations subcommittee that allocated defense spending, was found to have raked in $2.4 million by the time he was caught in 2005.

Cunningham, who referred to his enemies as "homos" and "socialists," was notably hard on drug dealers, voting for the death penalty for major dealers and deriding judges and politicians who supported light penalties for drugs, saying ""those who peddle destruction on our children must pay dearly." Months later he tearfully begged a judge for leniency after his son pleaded guilty to helping transport 400 pounds of marijuana.

Corruption always inspires conflicting loyalties. Consider the case of West Virginia Governor Wally Barron, indicted for establishing a network of dummy corporations to which vendors could funnel kickbacks. In a small state, rumors abounded. Residents gossiped that Barron, for example, had ordered all-new office furniture for government buildings, despite the fact that the furniture had just recently been replaced. After receiving a cut of the sale, truckloads of the brand-new furniture, lore had it, was taken to a rural bluff and dumped over the edge.

Barron was acquitted of these charges, perhaps because his wife slipped the jury foreman $25,000 in cash. The former governor, always careful to keep an arms distance between himself and shady deals, pleaded guilty to bribery, but said he was doing so not because of guilt, but to protect his wife. That chivalry cost him 4 years in the pen.

At the time of writing this book, this is Wikipedia's entry on Barron: In 1960 he was elected governor of West Virginia and set about attempting to undo the clean government and civil rights reforms that had been instituted by his predecessor Cecil H. Underwood. The West Virginia encyclopedia, however, congratulates Barron because "[he] achieved a remarkable record of legislative success during his term, brought national attention to Appalachia, and launched job programs in an era of high unemployment [and] firmly told Governor George Wallace of Alabama that he would oppose 'any and all statements . . . which would in any way promote or sanction discrimination.'" The truth doubtless lies somewhere in between.

In a state that at the time never elected Republicans, Republican Cecil Underwood was elected to office in 1956 when a week before the election it was discovered that Democratic US Rep. Robert Mollohan had received $20,000 and 2 cars from a coal operator on a strip mine at a state reformatory while Mollohan was the institution's superintendent. Underwood's first act as governor was to appear on the new invention of television and fire all state employees, who he said had been hired under corrupt Democratic machine-politics. Underwood, the youngest governor in state history, was the first contestant on the television game show *To Tell the Truth*. When reelected in 1997, he also became the state's oldest elected governor.

Former Louisiana Governor Edwin Edwards, whose political career began in the 1970s, was both corrupt and hard to catch.

Through his time in politics he beat 24 separate corruption charges before he was convicted on 17 counts of extorting money from casinos seeking government licenses. This seemed to surprise Edwards who once said the only thing that could bring him down was "if I'm caught in bed with either a dead girl or a live boy."

For those into analytics, the record for American political corruption would seem to rest with New York's William M. "Boss" Tweed, whose estimated $200 million in ill-gotten gains translates into a modern sum in excess of $4 billion. In the mid-1800s Tweed ruled the legendary Tammany Hall machine in New York City at a time when immigrants who stepped off the boat were given a plate of food, a place to live, a job, and strict instructions to vote Democratic.

> Tweed got his start in the ranks of volunteer fire companies, which were as much competing social and political entities as they were public service organizations. Sometimes entire buildings would burn while two competing companies would brawl in the street.

After taking control of the city under a new charter (the product of $600,000 in bribes), Tammany's methods to the accumulation of wealth were straightforward. Contractors and vendors doing business with the city were told to inflate their bills, and Tweed and Co. split the difference. Tweed once bought 300 benches at $5 each and resold them to the city for $600 per bench.

Tammany Hall was done in by a parade in which Irish Protestants and Catholics clashed and 60 people were killed. The ring's power came into question, and a clean-government crusade on the part of cartoonist Thomas Nast and *The New York Times* began to take hold. Of the two, Tweed was more concerned about the cartoonist. Because his constituents for the most part couldn't read, he didn't fear the newspaper articles, but he worried himself sick over the "damned pictures." A "Committee of Seventy" wrested control of Tammany by cutting off the city's funding—interrupting bond sales and refusing to pay taxes. City works revolted when they went unpaid.

Tweed was convicted of more than 200 counts of corruption in 1873. He escaped from jail, and fled to Spain where he went to work as a common sailor on a Spanish ship. He was recaptured when authorities recognized his face from Thomas Nast's cartoons in the *Times*. Tweed died in jail.

Occasionally, the making of legislation does not take place within the walls of the Capitol, but within the walls of corporate

America. In 2013, *The New York Times* reported that a bill easing banking regulations had in fact been largely formulated, not by lawmakers, but by Citigroup. According to the *Times*, "Two crucial paragraphs, prepared by Citigroup in conjunction with other Wall Street banks, were copied nearly word for word."

> ## Worldwide, an estimated $1 trillion in bribes changes hands each year.

A group, Tackling Corruption Together, that tracks corruption around the world says the most corrupt nations are Somalia, North Korea, and Afghanistan. The least corrupt are Denmark, Finland, Sweden, and New Zealand. Another group, Transparency International, puts its money (or wouldn't put its money) on Bangladesh, where it's estimated that 6 percent of the nation's GDP is spent on bribery.

In 1980s Chicago, money was no object for those seeking justice, or injustice, in the Cook County judicial system. Under Operation Greylord, authorities for more than 3 years investigated and arrested 93 people, including 17 judges, 48 lawyers, 10 deputy sheriffs, 8 policemen, 8 court officials, and 1 state lawmaker.

One reputed law-and-order judge, Thomas Maloney, was convicted in 1993 of fixing 3 murder cases for bribes of more than $100,000. Defense lawyers looking to fix the verdict reported that Maloney was dependable, but expensive.

If Thomas Maloney kept people out of prison, former Tennessee Governor Ray Blanton, elected to office in 1975, helped them out once they got in. His pardon of a man convicted in a double murder raised eyebrows after it was discovered that the killer's father had been one of Blanton's county campaign chairmen.

The heat caused Blanton not to seek reelection, but as the days of his term wound down, he went on a suspected pardon-for-profit spree, freeing 24 convicted murderers and 28 other criminals, including the son of a supporter who had killed his ex-wife and her companion. On issuing the pardon, Blanton congratulated himself, saying "this takes guts." The Tennessee Secretary of State retorted "Some people have more guts than brains."

Afraid that Blanton would pardon even more criminals in his last days in office, state officials found a loophole in the State Constitution that allowed them to swear in his replacement 3 days early.

> **Blanton was never charged with selling pardons, but he was charged with selling liquor licenses.**

Marie Ragghianti, chairwoman of the state Board of Prisons and Paroles, was fired by Blanton when she refused to release prisoners he had pardoned. Her story was later made into a motion picture, and her attorney played himself on the film, thereby launching the acting career of eventual US Sen. Fred Thompson.

Blanton, like many other public scofflaws, did some good. He brought tax relief to the elderly, was one of the first governors to recognize the economic value of tourism, and traveled overseas (if a bit too lavishly) to bring new business back to his home state.

In a similar vein, Zine Al-Abidine Ben Ali, former president of Tunisia, who served from 1987 to 2011, tripled his nation's per capita GDP, grew the Tunisian economy an average of 5 percent a year for 2 decades, and cut his nation's poverty rate in half, so perhaps he felt entitled to a little something for the effort. But that little something amounted to an estimated $2 billion, or there-abouts, that he is alleged to have stolen from the government. When he fled the country as the noose tightened, authorities seized from Ben Ali's extended family 550 properties, 40 stock portfolios, 367 bank accounts, 400 businesses, and 48 boats.

In 2010 Tunisia a 26-year-old fruit seller, for whom economic progress was not coming fast enough, publicly set himself on fire, touching off the Middle Eastern movement that became known as the Arab Spring.

Political patronage has been a way of life in American politics since the beginning of our nation. The White House used to be a relatively open place, where people could come to sit and wait for a word with the President, which they would often get. In the course of the conversation, they would helpfully remind the president that they had been a solid supporter for his campaign, and maybe the support was worth a little something in terms of a government job. Many a postmaster owed his position to backing the winning politician.

In their biography of President Lincoln, Nicolay and John Hay described how insane this process could be. Following Lincoln's election, "The city was full of strangers; the White House full of applicants from the North. At any hour of the day one might see at the outer door and on the staircase, one line going, one coming. In the anteroom and in the broad corridor adjoining the President's office there was a restless and persistent crowd—ten, twenty—sometimes fifty, varying with the day and hour, each one in pursuit of one of the many crumbs of official patronage. They walked the floor; they talked in groups; they scowled at every arrival and blessed every departure; they wrangled with the doorkeepers for the right of entrance; they intrigued with them for surreptitious chances; they crowded forward to get even as much as an instant's glance through the half-opened door into the Executive Chamber."

If it didn't work, of course, they wouldn't do it. Often the patronage involved work performed for political campaigns, but not always. When Louisiana Governor Huey Long proposed a tax hike on oil production, the friends of oil in the legislature discovered a number of offenses for which they said Long should be impeached—probably, it should be said, with some justification.

But Long chatted up a third of the Senate, the number necessary to block any conviction, and got them to sign a letter affirming that pursuing impeachment was useless, because they would not vote to convict under any circumstances. The senators were later rewarded with plum state jobs or, barring that, straight cash.

Long announced in 1935 that he would be a candidate for US President. He was shot to death a month later.

★

The lengths that some rulers will go to in order to protect their people can be heartwarming. In 2003, Teodoro Obiang Nguema Mbasogo, president of Equatorial Guinea declared that he believed the national treasury of his country was not safe from the corruption of government employees, so he seized control of his country's funds, $600 million of which he transferred to his own private bank account in the United States.

★

The US had broken off diplomatic relations with the West African nation in 1994 a year after Mbasogo accused an American diplomat, who had been honoring the graves of British airmen lost in WWII, of witchcraft. Relations were patched up in 2006, after the US discovered the extent of Equatorial Guinea's oil reserves.

In 1971, the US estimated that 64 percent of Haiti's budget had been misappropriated by Jean-Claude "Baby Doc" Duvalier.

No list of corruption would be complete without an item from Nigeria, and strongman Sani Abacha will serve as well as any. Abacha raised the coup d'état to an art form, having participated in no fewer than 4. In 1993 he assumed power himself, elevating his government above the court system, surrounding his palace with 3,000 bodyguards, coopting the military, banning political dissent, and taking charge of the press. Abacha did manage to improve Nigeria's overall economic outlook, probably because, like the familiar Nigerian emailer, he was always parking cash in foreign bank accounts in exchange for a minimal reinvestment. In all, Abacha is thought to have embezzled up to $5 billion, which he stashed in overseas banks. The dictator died of a heart attack in 1998, and his family, to avoid prosecution, has seen to the repatriation of much of the embezzled funds to Nigeria—where, bankers believe, much of it was re-stolen by newer corrupt Nigerian leaders.

Another African plotter, Mobutu Sese Seko Koko Ngbendu wa za Banga (best name meaning ever: "the all-powerful warrior who, because of endurance and an inflexible will to win, will go from conquest to conquest leaving fire in his wake") assumed power in Zaire—modern-day Congo—during a 1960 coup. Mobutu managed massive corruption without the added burden of improving his country at the same time. Thirty years into his rule, inflation stood at 4,000 percent. After 32 years, he was finally chased from office, but not before embezzling between $4 and $5 billion. His wise counsel to his colleagues in office was, "if you steal, do not steal too much at a time. You may be arrested. Steal cleverly, little by little."

These African tyrants learned from the best: their colonial European forbearers. Prior to Europe's colonization of Africa, which began in the latter half of the 19th century, corruption in Africa was relatively rare.

Watergate, the scandal that took down Richard Nixon and got its name from a Washington, D.C. hotel complex, touched off a series of other "gates," to the point that nary a whiff of corruption could drift across the capital—or anywhere—without the suffix "gate" being attached to it. There was Whitewatergate, Deavergate, Travelgate, Nannygate, Troopergate, even Deflategate, as it was applied to professional football.

> But perhaps the most amusing of the gates was Rubbergate, an episode in the 1990s where it was revealed that members of Congress habitually bounced checks drawn on the House of Representatives in-house bank.

The checks did not bounce in the traditional sense in that they were honored by the House bank in something along the lines of overdraft protection, albeit with no fees and no financial security, such as a line of credit. A full 450 Representatives were revealed to have, at the very least, taken advantage of the system, and 22 were singled out for chronic abuse of the system, with 1 member bouncing nearly 1,000 checks.

To the American public, this was everything that was wrong with Congress, whose members couldn't even handle their own finances, much less the nation's. Since the House was in Democratic hands, they were the ones who paid the price, being ushered out of power by Representative Newt Gingrich's "Republican Revolution."

Gingrich and his cohorts made much of the scandal, with 1 member even giving a speech on the House floor with a paper bag over his head to signify congressional shame. It turned out that Gingrich himself had overdrawn 22 checks, including a $9,462 check to the Internal Revenue Service.

It will probably come as no surprise that even Vatican City is not immune from corruption. Under Pope Leo X in the early 1500s, worshippers paid for their sins not with penance, but with cash. Leo had a full menu of sins, and the cost of absolution. But Leo needed a way to pay for the art, music, and luxuries he loved. He was, according to some, a hedonist in Pope's clothing.

He enjoyed pursuits that were considered beneath the dignity of a pope, including boar hunting and practical jokes. When the money he received from the states and from his selling of indulgences didn't produce enough cash, he had something of a papal yard sale, selling everything from cardinal hats to table settings to statues of the apostles.

When the Cold War ended and the Iron Curtain of secrecy fell, many Eastern European citizens were shocked at the level of government corruption from which they had previously been shielded. In 1989 reporters were invited to tour the residence of a Communist official (who had ostensibly been living in austerity) to find "a swimming pool, a greenhouse, gardeners, maids, a tailor, a beauty parlor, and a store with consumer goods unavailable to the general public." Communist officials were discovered to have vast hunting preserves, and in one case a 4.4-mile paved road led to a reclusive lodge—in a country where few public roads were adequately serviced.

BIBLIOGRAPHY

CHAPTER—ON THE CAMPAIGN TRAIL

Burke, Jason. "Coconut detained in Maldives over vote-rigging claims," *The Guardian*. 6 September, 2013. theguardian.com/world/2013/sep/06/coconut-detained-maldives-vote-rigging.

The Paradox of Mass Politics: Knowledge and Opinion in the American Electorate W. Russell Neuman. Cambridge: Harvard University Press, 1986.

"Joe Walsh," *Songfacts*. www.songfacts.com/facts/joe-walsh.

Dalleck, Robert. "Three News Revelations about LBJ," *The Atlantic*. April, 1998. theatlantic.com/magazine/archive/1998/04/three-new-revelations-about-lbj/377094/.

Tolchin, Martin. "How Johnson Won Election He'd Lost." *The New York Times*, 11 February 1990. nytimes.com/1990/02/11/us/how-johnson-won-election-he-d-lost.html.

Baltz, Dan. "The Mystery Of Ballot Box 13." *Washington Post*, 4 March 1990. washingtonpost.com/archive/entertainment/books/1990/03/04 /the-mystery-of-ballot-box-13/70206359-8543-48e3-9ce2- f3c4fdf6da3d/?utm_term=.4b9688e7251a.

Cutler, William G. *History of the State of Kansas*, A.T. Andreas, (1883), "Territorial History, Part 8".

Chan, Melissa. "3-year-old becomes Minnesota town's newest and youngest mayor." *New York Daily News*, 11 August 2015, nydailynews .com/news/national/3-year-old-minnesota-town-youngest -mayor-article-1.2321879.

CHAPTER 2—THE POLITICS OF AMERICAN DEMOCRACY

Chernow, Ron. "George Washington: The Reluctant President." *The Smithsonian*, February, 2011. smithsonianmag.com/history/george -washington-the-reluctant-president-49492/.

Schwartz, Rafi. "We Asked ICE About the Prank Calls to Their Anti-Immigrant Hotline and They Kind of Lost Their Shit." *Splinternews*, 4 April 2017. splinternews.com/we-asked-ice-about -the-prank-calls-to-their-anti-immigr-1794701252.

Wood, Gordon (2009). *Empire of Liberty: A History of the Early Republic, 1789–1815*. New York: Oxford University Press. p. 285.

Chernow, Ron *Alexander Hamilton*. New York: Penguin Books, 2005.

Levinson, Sanford. "The Twelfth Amendment." National Con-stitutional Center. constitutioncenter.org/interactive-constitution /amendments/amendment-xii.

Nathan L. Colvin and Edward B. Foley, *The Twelfth Amendment: A Constitutional Ticking Time Bomb*, 64 U. Miami L. Rev. 475, 2010. repository.law.miami.edu/umlr/vol64/iss2/5.

"The First Two Senators: An Odd Couple." The United States Senate. senate.gov/artandhistory/history/minute/The_First_Two_Senators _An_Odd_Couple.htm.

"The First Cornerstone." The Architect of the Capitol. aoc.gov/first -cornerstone.

Dunsing, Mariah. "The First Presidential Veto." Teaching American History, 8 April 2013. http://teachingamericanhistory.org/past -programs/hfotw/120408-2/.

CHAPTER 3—MONEY POLITICS

Rice, Dr, Alan. "The economic basis of the slave trade." Revealing Histories. revealinghistories.org.uk/how-did-money-from-slavery-help -develop-greater-manchester/articles/the-economic-basis-of-the -slave-trade.html.

Nix, Elizabeth. "7 Things You May Not Know About the Medicis." *History*, 16 November 2016. history.com/news/7-things-you-may -not-know-about-the-medicis.

Davdison, Jacob. "Money Lessons From the Presidents." *Money*, Time, Inc., 13 February 2016. time.com/money/3707291/financial -lessons-washington-lincoln-money/.

Michael, Geoffrey. "Money And Politics." *Investopedia*. investopedia .com/articles/economics/12/money-and-politics.asp.

"West Virginia Bridge Being Built Without Russian Aid." *Ocala Star-Banner*, 1 January 1980. news.google.com/newspapers?id=Og0 wAAAAIBAJ&sjid=sgUEAAAAIBAJ&pg=2235%2C462258.

"Money-in-Politics Timeline." *OpenSecrets.org*, Center for Responsive Politics. opensecrets.org/resources/learn/timeline.

Prokop, Andrew. "40 charts that explain money in politics." *Vox*, Vox Media, 30 July 2014. vox.com/2014/7/30/5949581/money -in-politics-charts-explain.

Lopes, Marina. "Brazil's top politicians are getting busted with literal suitcases full of cash." The Washington Post, 7 September 2017. washingtonpost.com/news/worldviews/wp/2017/09/07/brazils -top-politicians-are-literally-getting-busted-with-suitcases-full-of -cash/?utm_term=.3b2598becfd7.

Brown, Mary. "6 Outrageous Political Earmarks." *Investopedia*, 15 April 2010. investopedia.com/financial-edge/0410/6-outrageous -political-earmarks.aspx.

DiLallo, Matthew. "What is the Richest Country in the World? (Hint: It's Not America)." *The Motley Fool*, 24 June, 2015. fool.com /investing/general/2015/06/24/what-is-the-richest-country-in -the-world-hint-it-2.aspx.

Sameen. "25 Most Expensive Wars In History." *List 25*, 7 July 2015. list25.com/25-most-expensive-wars-in-history-2/.

Tully, Shawn. "5 Things You Need to Know About the $400 Million America Sent to Iran." *Fortune*, Time Inc., 5 August 2016. fortune.com/2016/08/05/money-america-iran/.

Maples, C.W. "Civil War Cotton Conspiracy or Follow the Money." *Civil War Bummer*, 4 April 2014. civilwarbummer.com/civil-war-cotton-conspiracy-or-follow-the-money/.

Gordon, John Steel. "How the Civil War United Our Money." *Barrons*, Dow Jones Network, 19 January 2013. barrons.com/articles/SB50001424052748703596604578235552788285428.

"The House Club Sandwich Debate." *History, Art & Archives*, United States House of Representatives. history.house.gov/HistoricalHighlight/Detail/36758?ret=True.

Specia, Megan. "'A Dumb Decision': US Said to Waste $28 Million on Afghan Army Camouflage." *The New York Times*, 21 June, 2017. nytimes.com/2017/06/21/world/asia/afghanistan-army-uniform-camouflage.html.

Sullivan, Laura. "Government's Empty Buildings Are Costing Taxpayers Billions." *All Things Considered*, National Public Radio, 12 March 2014. npr.org/2014/03/12/287349831/governments-empty-buildings-are-costing-taxpayers-billions.

"Election Overview." *OpenSecrets.org*, Center for Responsive Politics. opensecrets.org/overview/index.php?cycle=2018&display=T&type=A.

Koerth-Baker, Maggie. "How Money Affects Elections." *FiveThirtyEight*, ABC News Internet Ventures, 10 September 2018. fivethirtyeight.com/features/money-and-elections-a-complicated-love-story/?ex_cid=story-twitter.

CHAPTER 4—POLITICAL ANIMALS

"The Milton Mule." *Museum of Hoaxes*, hoaxes.org/archive/permalink /the_milton_mule.

Alexander, Radu. "10 Animals That Actually Held Political Office." *All That's Interesting*, 15 March 2015. allthatsinteresting.com/10 -animals-that-actually-held-political-office/2.

Stamp, Jimmy. "Political Animals: Republican Elephants and Democratic Donkeys." *Smithsonian.com*, Smithsonian Institution, 23 October 2013. smithsonianmag.com/arts-culture/political-animals -republican-elephants-and-democratic-donkeys-89241754/.

"Calvin Coolidge." Presidential Pet Museum, presidentialpetmuseum .com/presidents/30cc/.

Trickey, Erick. "Move over, Trump. This president's two lions set off the greatest emoluments debate." *The Washington Post*, 25 July 2017, washingtonpost.com/news/retropolis/wp/2018/07/22/move -over-trump-this-presidents-two-lions-were-the-center-of -the-greatest-emoluments-debate/?utm_term=.34893ea54ee6.

"FDR's re-election & the Fala Speech." *Pets in Politics*, 12 July 2010, petsinpolitics.blogspot.com/2010/07/fdrs-re-election-fala -speech.html.

Sudakov, Dmitry. "USSR's five amazing top secret projects that were shelved." *Pravda*, PRAVDA.Ru, 23 December 2016, pravdareport.com /society/stories/23-12-2016/136500-soviet_secret_projects-0 /Gee, Allison. "Pushinka: A Cold War puppy the Kennedys loved." BBC, 6 January 2014, bbc.com/news/magazine-24837199.

Sebastian, Nick. "10 Fascinating Pets Of Powerful World Leaders." *Listverse*, Listverse Ltd, 10 April 2014, listverse.com/2014/04/10/10 -fascinating-pets-of-powerful-world-leaders/.

CHAPTER 5—POLITICAL SECRETS

Sass, Erik. "Secret Cities of the Soviet Union." Mental Floss, 28 March 2008, mentalfloss.com/article/18319/secret-cities-soviet -union.

Gage, Beverly. "The Strange Politics of 'Classified' Information." *The New York Times Magazine*, The New York Times, 22 August 2017, nytimes.com/2017/08/22/magazine/the-strange-politics-of-classified-information.html.

Memmott, Mark. "CIA Reveals Six Oldest Classified Documents; Now We Can All Read Them." *The Two-Way*, National Public Radio, 20 April 2011, npr.org/sections/thetwo-way/2011/04/20/135564718 /cia-reveals-its-six-oldest-classified-documents-now-we-can -all-read-them.

Weiss, Philip. "Masters of the Universe Go to Camp: Inside the Bohemian Grove." *Spy Magazine*, November 1989, cited whorulesamerica .ucsc.edu/power/bohemian_grove_spy.html.

Miller, Greg. "The Soviet Military Program that Secretly Mapped the Entire World." *National Geographic*, National geographic Society, 13 October 2017, news.nationalgeographic.com/2017/10/maps -soviet-union-ussr-military-secret-mapping-spies/.

Littlefield, Henry. "The Wizard of Oz: Parable on Populism." *American Quarterly*, The Johns Hopkins University Press, Spring 1964, https://www.jstor.org/stable/2710826?seq=1#page_scan_tab_contents.

Wolf, Jim. "Pentagon Planned 1960s Cuban 'Terror Campaign'," *Reuters*, 18 November 1997.

Blitz, Matt. "The Real Story Behind The Myth Of Area 51." *Popular Mechanics*, Hearst Communications, 14 September 2017, popularmechanics.com/military/research/a24152/area-51-history/.

Gorvet, Zavia. "The Ghostly Radio Station That No One Claims To Run." BBC, 2 August 2017, bbc.com/future/story/20170801-the-ghostly-radio-station-that-no-one-claims-to-run.

Daughtery, Greg. "Two Pilots Saw a UFO. Why Did the Air Force Destroy the Report?" *History*, 16 August 2018, history.com/news/ufo-chiles-whitted-soviet-spycraft-air-force-coverup.

Schoenberg, Tom. "CIA Cover-Up Suit Over Scientist's Fatal Fall Dismissed." *Bloomberg News*, 17 July 2013, bloomberg.com/news/articles/2013-07-17/cia-cover-up-suit-over-scientist-s-fatal-fall-dismissed.

Griffen, Andrew. "Wikileaks Cia Files: The 6 Biggest Spying Secrets Revealed By The Release Of 'Vault 7'." *The Independent*, 7 March 2017, independent.co.uk/life-style/gadgets-and-tech/news/wikileaks-cia-what-are-they-explained-vault-7-year-zero-julian-assange-secrets-a7616826.html.

Wise, David. "The CIA Burglar Who Went Rogue." *Smithsonian*, Smithsonian Institution, October 2012, smithsonianmag.com/history/the-cia-burglar-who-went-rogue-36739394/.

McFadden, Christopher. "The Russian Woodpecker: The Soviet Signal That Could Be Heard on the Radio." *Interesting Engineering*, 12 January 2018, interestingengineering.com/the-russian-woodpecker-the-soviet-signal-that-could-be-heard-on-the-radio.

Volkman, Ernest. *The History of Espionage*. London: Carlton Books Ltd., 2007.

"Top 10 Weird Government Secrets." *Time*, Time, Inc., /content.time.com/time/specials/packages/article/0,28804,2008962_2008964_2008982,00.html.

Smolkin, Rachel and Williams, Brenna. "How LBJ scared visitors at his ranch." *CNN*, Cable News Network, cnn.com/interactive/2015/10/politics/lbj-ranch-history/.

Gardham, Duncan. "MI6 attacks al-Qaeda in 'Operation Cupcake'." *The Telegraph*, Telegraph Media Group, 2 June 2011, telegraph.co.uk/news/uknews/terrorism-in-the-uk/8553366/MI6-attacks-al-Qaeda-in-Operation-Cupcake.html.

"Advisory Committee on Human Radiation Experiments" Final Report." United States.Advisory Committee on Human Radiation Experiments. Washington: Joseph Henry Press, 1995, archive.org/stream/advisorycommitte00unit/advisorycommitte00unit_djvu.txt.

Pearson, Drew. "Air Force Hires Nazi Doctor Linked to Ghastly Experiments." *Free Lance-Star*, 14 February 1952, news.google.com/newspapers?nid=1298&dat=19520214&id=V9NNAAAAIBAJ&sjid=dYoDAAAAIBAJ&pg=1786,4593995.

"Project Mockingbird: Spying on Reporters." *New York Times Blog*, The New York Times Company, 26 June 2007, washington.blogs .nytimes.com/2007/06/26/project-mockingbird/

Anthony, Carl. "Edith Wilson: The First, First Lady President." *Biography*, A & E Television Network, 10 March 2016, biography .com/news/edith-wilson-first-president-biography-facts

CHAPTER 6—THE POLITICS OF LEGISLATION

Bomboy, Scott. "Five 'unusual' amendments that never made it into the Constitution." *Constitution Daily*, National Constitution Center, 23 February 2018, constitutioncenter.org/blog/five-unusual -amendments-that-never-made-it-into-the-constitution.

"Rules and Manners." Washington Metropolitan Area Transit Authority, .wmata.com/rider-guide/rules/.

"No. 15. An Act Relating To Designating The State Pie And The State Fruit." 10 My 1999. leg.state.vt.us/docs/2000/acts/ACT015.HTM.

"Social Security." *Now*, PBS, 4 February 2005, pbs.org/now/politics /socialsechistory.html.

Frankel, Matthew. "12 Facts About Social Security You Didn't Know." The Motley Fool, 10 October, 2017, fool.com/retirement/2017 /10/10/12-facts-about-social-security-you-didnt-know.aspx.

"Help America Vote Act." The US Election Assistance Commission, eac.gov/about/help-america-vote-act/.

"Legal Curiosities: Fact or Fable?" Law Commission, UK. Internet Archive. April 2015, web.archive.org/web/20150629195445/http://lawcommission.justice.gov.uk/docs/Legal_Oddities.pdf.

CHAPTER 7—THE POLITICS OF SEX

"Top 10 Unfortunate Political One-Liners." *Time*, Time, Inc. content.time.com/time/specials/packages/article/0,28804, 1859513_1859526_1859518,00.html.

Joyner, James. "Bill Clinton, Mark Foley and Sexless Sex." Outside the Beltway, 14 October 2006, outsidethebeltway.com /bill_clinton_mark_foley_and_sexless_sex/.

Robson, James. "The truth about sex in ancient Greece." *The Conversation*, 1 April 2015, theconversation.com/the-truth-about-sex-in-ancient -greece-39025.

Holmen, Nicole. "Examining Greek Pederastic Relationships." *Inquiries*, Inquiries Journal/Student Pulse LLC, 2010 Vol. 2 No. 02 | Pg. 1/1, inquiriesjournal.com/articles/175/examining-greek-pederastic -relationships.

Suetonius. "The Life of Tiberius." *The Lives of the Caesars*, Loeb Classical Library, 1913, uchicago.edu/Thayer/E/Roman/Texts/Suetonius /12Caesars/Tiberius*.html

Remini, Robert. *Daniel Webster: The Man and His Time*. New York" W. W. Norton & Company, 1997.

Tribune News Services. "Gingrich Friend Dates Affair To '93." *Chicago Tribune*. 11 November 1999, chicagotribune.com/news/ct-xpm -1999-11-11-9911110139-story.html.

Rudin, Ken. "Congressional Sex Scandals in History." *The Washington Post*, washingtonpost.com/wp-srv/politics/special/clinton/congress .htm.

Hanton, Alex. "10 Sex Scandals That Shocked The Ancient World." *ListVerse*, 22 October 2016, listverse.com/2016/10/22/10 -sex-scandals-that-shocked-the-ancient-world/.

CHAPTER 8—THE POLITICS OF VIOLENCE

Holodney, Elena and Macias, Amanda. "The 25 most ruthless leaders of all time." *Business Insider*, 7 Octobr 2015, businessinsider. com/most-ruthless-leaders-of-all-time-2015-10.

Genghis Khan. *History*, A&E Television, history.com/topics/genghis -khan.

May, Radmila. "The Battle of Great Severn." *Contemporary Review*, March 1999.

Blakemore, Erin. "California's Little-known Genocide." *History*, A&E Television, history.com/news/californias-little-known-genocide.

Gettleman, Jeffrey. "Lessons From the Barbary Pirate Wars." *The New York Times*, 11 April 2009, nytimes.com/2009/04/12/weekinreview /12gettleman.html.

CHAPTER 9—POLITICAL DIRTY TRICKS

"*Colonial Manners: Based on the Exercise of a Schoolboy*" (Washington, George. "Rules of Civility & Decent Behaviour In Company and

Conversation"). The Colonial Williamsburg Foundation, history .org/almanack/life/manners/rules2.cfm.

McClatchy Newspapers. "Hotheaded presidents." *Seattle Times*, 8 September 2008, seattletimes.com/seattle-news/politics/hotheaded -presidents/.

"5 People Who Threw Shade on George Washington." New England Historical Society. newenglandhistoricalsociety.com/5-people-threw-shade -george-washington/.

AP Photo. "16-worst-political-dirty-tricks: John McCain's 'other child.'" *Politico*, 16 June 2012, politico.com/gallery/2012/06/16 -worst-political-dirty-tricks/000188-002249-fullscreen.html.

Krieg, Gregory. "The 10 weirdest political stories of 2015, not including Trump." CNN Politics, Cble News Network, 29 December 2015, cnn.com/2015/12/22/politics/2015-weird-political -stories/index.html.

Will, George F. "Briefing Book Baloney." *The Washington Post*. p. A23, 11 August, 2005.

Grossman, Mark. *Political Corruption in America: An Encyclopedia of Scandals, Power, and Greed*. Amenia, NY: Grey House Publishing, 2008.

Schulz, Colin. "Nixon Prolonged Vietnam War for Political Gain—And Johnson Knew About It, Newly Unclassified Tapes Suggest." *Smithsonian*, Smithsonian Institution, 18 March 2013, smithsonianmag.com/smart-news/nixon-prolonged-vietnam-war -for-political-gainand-johnson-knew-about-it-newly-unclassified -tapes-suggest-3595441/.

CHAPTER 10—WOMEN IN POLITICS

Lamb, Martha. *History of the City of New York*. New York: A.S. Barnes & Company, 1877, books.google.com/books?id=d0M4AQAAMAAJ &pg=PA160#v=onepage&q&f=false%20She-Paul%20Revere.

Mangiola, Sarah. "Marita Lorenz: The Spy Who Loved Castro . . . and Almost Assassinated Him." *The Archive*, Open Road Media, 10 October 2017, explorethearchive.com/marita-lorenz-the-spy-who -loved-castroand-almost-assassinated-him.

"Hoda Shaarawy." Wikepedia, wikipedia.org/wiki/Huda_Sha%27arawi.

Maranzani, Barbara. "8 Things You Didn't Know About Catherine the Great." *History*, A & E Television Networks, 9 July, 2012, history. com/news/8-things-you-didnt-know-about-catherine-the-great.

Oh, Su and Kliff, Sarah. "The US is ranked 104th in women's representation in government." *Vox*, Vox Media, 8 March 2017, vox.com/identities/2017/3/8/14854116/women-representation.

The Editors of Encyclopaedia Britannica. "Lola Montez, Irish Dancer." *Encyclopaedia Britannica*, britannica.com/biography/ Lola-Montez.

CHAPTER 11—THE POLITICS OF TAXATION

"11 Strange State Tax Laws." TurboTax, Intuit, 2017, turbotax.intuit. com/tax-tips/fun-facts/12-strange-state-tax-laws/L4qENY2nZ.

"Strange & Unusual Taxes Throughout History." Efile, efile.com /unusual-strange-funny-taxes-throughout-the-world-and-history/.

Andrews, William G. (1904). *At the Sign of the Barber's Pole: Studies in Hirsute History.* Cottingham, Yorkshire, J.R. Tutin, 1904.

Amadeo, Kimberly. "Sin Taxes, Their Pros and Cons, and Whether They Work." *The Balance,* Dotdash Publishing, 10 July 2018, thebalance.com/sin-tax-definition-examples-4157476.

Pace, Eric. "Cigarette Prices Tiptoe Higher." *The New York Times,* 2 November 1982, nytimes.com/1982/11/02/business/cigarette -prices-tiptoe-higher.html.

Marijuana Tax Data, Colorado Department of Revenue. colorado .gov/pacific/revenue/colorado-marijuana-tax-data.

Helvering, Guy T. "Intelligence Unit Bureau of Internal Revenue, Treasury Department: Organization, Functions and Activities, A Narrative Briefly DescriptiveOf the Period 1919 to 1936."

irs.gov/pub/irs-utl/file-5-intelligence-unit-narrative-of- period-1919-1936-by-guy-helvering.pdf.

Drenkard, Scott and Bishop-Henchman, Joseph. "Sales Tax Holidays: Politically Expedient but Poor Tax Policy, 2018. The Tax Foundation, 17 July 2018, taxfoundation.org/sales-tax-holidays -politically-expedient-poor-tax-policy-2018/.

"Historical Barriers to Voting." *Texas Politics,* University of Texas at Austin, 9 October 2018, Internet Archive, archive.org/web /20080402060131/http:/texaspolitics.laits.utexas.edu/html/vce /0503.html.

Jones-Branch, Cherisse. "'To Speak When and Where I Can': African American Women's Political Activism in South Carolina in the 1940s and 1950s." *The South Carolina Historical Magazine*. July 2016107 (3): 204–24.

"Five facts about Swiss bank secrecy."*Reuters*, Thomson Reuters, reuters.com/article/banking-secrecy/factbox-five-facts-about-swiss-bank-secrecy-idINLD24084820090313.

Hustad, Karis. "Top 12 weirdest tax rules around the world." CNBC, NBC Universal, 14 February 2014, cnbc.com/2014/02/14/top-12-weirdest-tax-rules-around-the-world.html.

Adrian. "3 Weird Stories For Tax Day." Ripley's Believe It or Not, Ripley Entertainment, 5 July 2018, ripleys.com/weird-news/tax-day/.

Fucoloro, Tom. "State lawmaker defends bike tax, says bicycling is not good for the environment." Seattle Bike Blog, 2 March 2013, seattlebikeblog.com/2013/03/02/state-lawmaker-says-bicycling-is-not-good-for-the-environment-should-be-taxed/.

Chopra, Isha. "Top 10 smallest countries in the world." Small Budget, Big Trips, smallbudgetbigtrips.com/top-10-smallest-countries-world/.

CHAPTER 12—THE POLITICS OF DRINK

MacAskill, Ewen. "I'll drink to that . . ." *The Guardian*, Guardian News and Media Limited, UK, 15 December 2000, theguardian.com/g2/story/0,3604,411605,00.html.

Kennedy, Geraldine "Yeltsin feels better after Shannon nap". *The Irish Times*, 1 October 1994.

"The Politics of Alcohol." The British Medical Journal, 5 January 1985, ncbi.nlm.nih.gov/pmc/articles/PMC1415345/pdf /bmjcredoo0428-0003.pdf.

Hutt, David, "Drinking in Hanoi: Alcohol and Politics in Vietnam." *The Diplomat*, 27 December 2017, thediplomat.com/2017/12/drinking -in-hanoi-alcohol-and-politics-in-vietnam/.

Lendler, Ian. *Alcoholica Esoterica*. New York: Penguin, 2005.

Yakovlev, Pavel and Guessford, Walter. "Alcohol Consumption and Political Ideology: What's Party Got to Do with It?" *Journal of Wine Economics*, Cambridge University Press, December 2013, cambridge .org/core/journals/journal-of-wine-economics/article/alcohol -consumption-and-political-ideology-whats-party-got-to-do -with-it/D7191B2F1C4F11D9527AFA6F06614912.

Riordon, William. Plunkitt of Tammany Hall: a series of very plain talks on very practical politics by George Washington Plunkitt. 1905, gutenberg.org/files/2810/2810-h/2810-h.htm#link2HCH0018.

Hanson, David. "Politicians and Alcohol Trivia: Fun Facts on Politics & Alcohol." Alcohol Problems and Solutions, Sociology Department, State University of New York, Potsdam, alcohol problemsandsolutions.org/politicians-and-alcohol-trivia-fun-facts -on-politics-alcohol/.

Hendricks, M. "Liquor laws live up to state motto." *Kansas City Star*, 7 April 2003.

"Presidential Vehicles." Lyndon B. Johnson National Historic Park Texas, National Park Service, nps.gov/lyjo/planyourvisit /presidentialvehicles.htm

Scowcroft/Kissinger, National Archives and Records Administration, Box 22, File 10, 11 October 1973, nsarchive2.gwu.edu//NSAEBB /NSAEBB123/Box%2022,%20File%2010,%20Scowcroft%20 -%20Kissinger%20oct%2011%2073%205,55%20pm%20089.pdf.

"A Complete Guide to the US Presidents and Their Drug and Alcohol Use." Project Know, American Addiction Centers, project know.com/a-complete-guide-to-the-us-presidents-and-their -drug-and-alcohol-use/.

"Health and Medical History of President Grover Cleveland." Doctor Zebra, doctorzebra.com/prez/g22.htm.

Wright, Ben. *Order, Order!: The Rise and Fall of Political Drinking.* Gerald Duckworth & Co. LTD (UK), 2016.

Peele, Stanton. "Where the Founding Fathers Alcoholics?" Life, Huffington Post, 17 November 2011, huffingtonpost.com/stanton -peele/alcohol-addiction-were-th_b_610598.html.

CHAPTER 13—THE POLITICS OF RELIGION

Historyplex Staff. "Bone-chilling Yet Interesting Facts About the Spanish Inquisition." 2 March 2018, historyplex.com/interesting -facts-about-spanish-inquisition.

Edwards, Owen. "How Thomas Jefferson Created His Own Bible." Smithsonian, Smithsonian Institution, January 2012, smithsonianmag .com/arts-culture/how-thomas-jefferson-created-his-own -bible-5659505?.

Morgan, Charles and Walker, Hubert. "In God We Trust: A Brief History." *Coinweek*, 22 April 2017, coinweek.com/us-coins/in -god-we-trust-a-brief-history/.

Goodstein, Laurie. "In Seven States, Atheists Push to End Largely Forgotten Ban." *The New York Times*, 6 December 2014, nytimes. com/2014/12/07/us/in-seven-states-atheists-push-to-end -largely-forgotten-ban-.html.

"French court bans Christ advert." BBC, 11 March 2005, bbc.co .uk/2/hi/europe/4337031.stm.

Chulov, Martin. "Qur'an etched in Saddam Hussein's blood poses dilemma for Iraq leaders." *The Guardian*, Guardian News and Media Limited, 19 December 2010, theguardian.com/world/2010/dec /19/saddam-legacy-quran-iraqi-government.

"25 Interesting Vatican City Facts. *Kickass Facts*, KickassFacts-Fact Encyclopedia, 22 December 2014, kickassfacts.com/25-interesting -vatican-city-facts/.

Rickard, J. "Siege of Isfizar, 1383." Military History Encyclopedia on the Web, 20 September 2010, http://www.historyofwar.org /articles/siege_isfizar.html.

Milwright, Marcus. "So Despicable a Vessel: Representations of Tamerlane in Printed Books of the Sixteenth and Seventeenth Centuries." *Muqarnas,* An Annual on the Visual Cultures of the Islamic World is sponsored by the Aga Khan Program for Islamic Architecture at Harvard University and the Massachusetts Institute of Technology, Cambridge, Massachusetts, 2006, jstor.org/ stable/25482447?seq=1#page_scan_tab_contents.

Strattton, Mark. "Uzbekistan: On the bloody trail of Tamerlane." *The Independent,* 9 July 2006, independent.co.uk/service/contact -us-759589.html.

Pongratz-Lippitt, Christa. "Austria's perilous journey." *The Tablet,* 9 November 2013, archive.is/MdIsW#selection-3247.8–3247.24.

Williams, T. Harry. *Huey Long.* New York: Vintage Books. 12 August 1981.

Lipka, Michael. "10 facts about religion in America." Fact Tank, Pew ResearchCenter, 27 August 2015, pewresearch.org/fact-tank /2015/08/27/10-facts-about-religion-in-america/.

CHAPTER 14—POLITICS AND CORRUPTION

Kabler, Phil. "Former Gov. Underwood dead." *Charleston Gazette,* 25 November 2008, web.archive.org/web/20081206021153/http: /www.wvgazette.com/News/200811241158.

Canfield, Jack. "William Wallace Barron." The West Virginia Encyclopedia, 16 May 2016, wvencyclopedia.org/articles/366.

Shukla, Vikas. "Top Ten Most Corrupt Politicians In The World." ValueWalk, 22 February 2018, valuewalk.com/2018/02/nawaz-sharif -most-corrupt-prime-minister/.

Cohn, Scott. "Meet America's Most Crooked Politicians." CNBC, NBC Universal, 28 July 2016, cnbc.com/2016/07/28/meet-americas -most-crooked-politicians.html.

Lipton, Eric and Protess, Ben. "Banks' Lobbyists Help in Drafting Financial Bills." *The New York Times*, 23 May 2013, nytimes.com /2013/05/23/banks-lobbyists-help-in-drafting-financial-bills/.

Hartson, William. "Top 10 facts about corruption." *Express,* Express Newspapers (UK), 12 May 2016, express.co.uk/life-style/top10facts /669514/top-ten-facts-corruption-Tackling-Corruption-Together -conference-London.

"Ten Most Corrupt Politicians." Real Clear Politics, Real Clear Holdings, realclearpolitics.com/lists/most_corrupt_politicians/rayblanton .html

Clymer, Adam. "House Revolutionary." The *New York Times*, 23 August 1992, nytimes.com/1992/08/23/magazine/house-revolutionary .html.

Melina, Remy. "7 Quite Unholy Pope Scandals." Live Science, 17 September 2010, livescience.com/8606-7-unholy-pope-scandals .html.

Binder, David. "Clamor in the East; Reports of Corruption in East Berlin Shock Even the Party Rank and File." *The New York Times,* 25 November 1989, nytimes.com/1989/11/25/world/clamor-east- reports-corruption-east-berlin-shock-even-party-rank-file.htm.

Murphy, Bill. "Son of lawmaker sentenced to prison." *The San Diego Union-Tribune,* 18 November 1998, http://dukecunningham.org /bibliography/drugs.html#19981118.